YOU
Belong

A Call for Connection

YOU
Belong

Sebene Selassie

HarperOne
An Imprint of HarperCollinsPublishers

HarperOne

HarperCollins books may be purchased for educational, business, or sales promotional use. For information, please email the Special Markets Department at SPsales@harpercollins.com.

FIRST EDITION

Designed by SBI Book Arts, LLC

Library of Congress Cataloging-in-Publication Data has been applied for.

ISBN 978-0-06-294065-0

20 21 22 23 24 LSC 10 9 8 7 6 5 4 3 2 1

CONTENTS

To my mother, Koki Menkir, for showing me the power of belonging

&

To Frederic, for showing me love is belonging

YOU
Belong

An Invitation to Belonging

At the age of thirty-four, while most of my girlfriends hurriedly made babies before their fertility windows closed, I received a diagnosis of stage three breast cancer.

I did not feel sick. I ate cleanly, biked to work, practiced yoga regularly, looked radiant, and my body was trying to kill me. Physically, I felt great. Emotionally, I was a mess. Recently broken up from my first long-term relationship, I returned to Washington, DC, where I had not lived since I was eighteen. People I knew were settling down in careers and first homes while I was in debt, living at my mom's, and working for a dysfunctional international organization. I longed to belong to life but I contemplated my death daily. That's when I started taking coffee up my butt.

I explored alternative treatments with a doctor at an integrative health center in Tenleytown. She used coffee enemas as part of a complex detoxification protocol. Every week for a year, cooled organic decaf arabica would flow through a tube into my rectum until it was full. After many minutes alone in the room (during which I sometimes sang to myself and usually failed to relax), a nurse would return and allow me to release my bowels. We would do this again three or four times each session.

Colonics have long been believed to detoxify the body. Around 1500 BCE, an ancient Egyptian medical document *Ebers papyrus* described the benefits of colon cleansing, and many traditional healing systems have some type of colonic irrigation. Coffee enemas are thought to detoxify the liver. Does it work? I'm not sure. At least it didn't hurt my recovery and wasn't painful.

Why is this relevant at the beginning of a book about belonging? Belonging is an expression of life. I would have done anything to belong to the living. Also, everything is relevant when we talk about belonging. The challenge with belonging in these times is "*everything*" includes a whole lot of things, including coffee poop. We live in a world where previously isolated languages, cultures, and beliefs have been melded into each other. Each of us has a multitude of influences, various identities, and countless experiences. Furthermore, things are bananas out there. We are presented with a dizzying array of choices every day—what to eat, use, read, watch, follow, post, support, say, believe—choices that align us with particular ideas, values, and communities . . . or not. In any moment, we may feel like we belong to one thing and not another. I belong to *this* community, to which others don't. I belong to *this* statement, definitely not that one. I belong in *this* space way over here. Or perhaps I belong nowhere. The truth: *we all belong to it all.* Also to death.

I did not tell most people about my coffee colonics (until now, when I'm telling absolutely everyone—hello there!). When I was first diagnosed, I chose to pursue only alternative treatments. My mother and our family friends, like many immigrants steeped in faith and traditional medicine and wary of Western (read: white) doctors, encouraged me to try natural therapies. The conventional doctors I was seeing and some friends disagreed with this decision. I was utterly unsure about my choices.

Eventually, I decided to combine allopathic and alternative medicines. Exploring both ancient and modern health systems, I often felt caught between them. This was fifteen years ago, and most cancer centers were only tiptoeing into integrating other modalities. I felt nervous about mentioning acupuncture to my oncologist. The fact that I included spiritual practice as part of my healing made me feel even more "far out." I never mentioned my devotional prayers to science-only, nonreligious friends, yet I was the one who felt skeptical when people made recommendations for miracle nutritional supplements or suggested that I could cure cancer through my thoughts. I was confused and navigating things my peers had not. I felt isolated and aberrant.

I don't wish cancer on anyone else, but I wouldn't change a thing about my experience. That doesn't mean it was easy: I wasn't always open to what was happening while it was happening. But the challenges I faced—the challenges you face, the challenges we face collectively at this time, any place in the world (even a colonic room), *any* challenge in life (even cancer)—all are invitations to belonging. And belonging is our true nature.

Belonging is our capacity to feel joy, freedom, and love in any moment. As the late Zen teacher Charlotte Joko Beck said: *Joy is exactly what's happening, minus our opinion of it.* She made a distinction between joy and happiness—Happiness has an opposite: unhappiness. Joy is not about happy or unhappy, liking or disliking. Joy is accepting each moment for what it is without contention. We belong to any moment simply by meeting it with joy. *This* is freedom. Love is the ultimate expression of joy and freedom. Joy, freedom, and love could be considered synonyms for each other, and for belonging.

I had longed to belong my entire life. I longed to fit in, I longed to achieve success, and I longed to have a soul mate. No one yearns to belong to cancer, especially not a single young woman searching for her purpose in life. Over the next ten years, I would have two recurrences of the disease, each more grave than the last. Cancer threatened my capacity to belong to anyone or anything—except that it didn't. It was my entry point. The truth is: we all have a 100 percent chance of dying. The only things human beings who breathe a breath have in common are birth, death, and belonging. Even in dying, we belong.

You belong. Period.

Not Belonging Is Only a Feeling

Belonging is not dependent on things being as we want them to be. It is not necessary to achieve (some definition of) success, behave like everyone else, have the perfect partner, be the perfect size or shape. In fact, the forces of oppression need not even magically disappear (though that would be cool) for us to experience belonging. And get this: we also don't need to *feel* belonging to belong. Belonging is truth and it is the fundamental nature of reality right here and now, whether we feel it or not. For me, it's often been *not*.

I explore belonging precisely because for most of my life I felt I did not belong anywhere—forget *everywhere*. I was plagued with feelings of not belonging no matter where I went. I have been writing this book for almost a year. I have been living this book my entire life. I'm sure I've longed to belong since before I can remember. I do remember being very young and unsure of where or who was home. I was a toddler when my family emigrated from Ethiopia in the early seventies (I am half Ethiopian and half Eritrean). I felt out of place in an American culture that was a lot less diverse than it is today and in an immigrant community that was much smaller than it is now. I grew up Black in white neighborhoods, and I didn't feel like I connected to any one racial culture. I was a girl who was not interested in girlie things (so, yes, on top of everything else, I was the *tomboy* Black immigrant girl).

"Difference" does not equal "not belonging," but as many of us live farther away from our families and as we connect to multiple communities and cultures, our sense of belonging feels tenuous. Race, gender, class, sexual orientation, ability, religion, ethnicity, culture, size, politics, profession, lifestyle, and even clothing can highlight differences that delineate borders between us that become (false) barriers to belonging. Into my thirties I assumed there were certain ways to be(long). I did not seem to get them. I was too blackish for the white folks. Not Black enough for the Black folks. Too Americanized to get my roots. Too immigrant to get American idioms. Too feminist for heels. Too femme not to do my brows. Too intellectual for the intuitives. Not sufficiently read for the academy. Too political for my party friends. Not radical enough for my activist friends. Too hetero to call myself queer. Too queer to care about most hetero nonsense. Too woo-woo for the skeptics. Not spiritual enough for the renunciates. I had too much money. Not enough.

Lifelong practice with feelings of not belonging has made me a belonging specialist. Almost everything I've pursued in life connects to this longing to belong. I majored in religious studies, feminism, race, and cultural studies searching for answers about belonging. I journaled, doodled, and made videos about belonging. I smoked it, drank it, popped it, and snorted it in an attempt to belong. I went to countless classes, seminars, and retreats chasing belonging. I practiced yoga and meditation, seeking out teachers in my quest to find belonging. I protested and petitioned to belong. I fasted and juiced to belong.

And now I work to help others remember their belonging. I've studied and practiced Buddhism for thirty years and have taught meditation for over a decade. I've trained in various modalities to help individuals and groups explore transformation and liberation. I teach workshops, courses, and retreats online and in person leading people to investigate what belonging means in our multicultural, modern reality. And I've been diagnosed with cancer three times, including twice with stage four metastatic cancer (there's no stage five), and am thankfully cancer free. Yet, even now, there are moments I feel I don't belong (sometimes I scroll, click, and post to feel like I belong).

My friend Nidhi describes not belonging like going to the mall gift shop every week and spinning the display with the personalized key rings, searching for your name even though you know you'll never find it. We search externally for belonging (hint: it's not out there). It took me time and practice to unlearn this outside searching, to understand that the key to belonging is within. Belonging is my nature: therefore, I belong everywhere and so does everyone else. Including you.

But at some point, in your life or in the past fifteen minutes, you have probably felt you don't belong. Maybe you felt insecure, angry, anxious, fearful, sad, disconnected, frustrated, or all of these things at once. It's not wrong to have these feelings come up. The only problem with feelings is thinking there's a problem with feelings. We mostly don't like unpleasant feelings and want to get rid of them.

You're not alone in feeling unpleasant feelings. There's a lot to feel unpleasant about (and a lot to which we don't want to belong). Hate crimes are on the rise in the US. Politics are polarized everywhere, with xenophobia and racism fueling a resurgence of populism across the world. A global pandemic halted life everywhere and altered all of our lives. Uprisings ignited across the world in defense of Black lives. Our planet is in severe environmental crisis and there is no agreed-upon remedy for the fact that we are hurtling toward destruction.

Feeling bad can make us feel worse. Anxiety and depression have skyrocketed among young people, affecting close to one in three young adults. Loneliness is at epidemic proportions as studies show that social isolation increases stress hormones and can even lead to illness and premature death. Though US rates are the highest, governments around the world (including Denmark, Japan, and Australia) are addressing loneliness as a crisis (and this was before corona shutdowns). The UK created an entire ministerial commission on it. While loneliness is exacerbated for older people by physical isolation, some speculate it plagues young people even more (influenced by, you guessed it, those gadgets in our pockets). Not belonging doesn't only affect people who are alone; one study shows that half of those reporting chronic loneliness are married people.

If we belong to it all, we all belong to this, too.

Be Longing

We are because we belong.
—ARCHBISHOP DESMOND TUTU

Do you believe it? Do you believe that you belong? Because you do. You belong. Everywhere. Yes, you—with all your history, anxiety, pain. Yes, everywhere—in every culture, community, circumstance. You belong in this body. You belong in this very moment. You belong in this breath . . . and this one. You have always belonged.

When you don't like the joke, you belong. When you're the "only one" of your race, disability, or sexuality, you belong. When you're terrified to speak in public, you belong. When you feel hurt or when you have hurt someone else you belong. When you are down to your last dollars and the rent is due, you belong. When you feel overwhelmed by the horrors of human beings, you belong. When you have a debilitating illness, you belong. When everyone else is getting married, you belong. When you don't know what you're doing with your life, you belong. When the world feels like it's falling apart, you belong. When you feel you don't belong, you belong.

Contemporary life makes it easy to forget belonging. My aspiration is that this book helps you remember that you belong in every moment, to everything, and then, like it or not, to every(damn)one. When I forget, I recall this: belonging is an imperative—*be longing*. Our desire to belong is what makes us human precisely because feeling like we don't belong opens us to belonging. If we didn't long for it, our species would have perished. Our longing to belong is, as Irish poet David Whyte says, one of our "core competencies."

Try it right now. Connect to any ways you feel you don't fit in, aren't accepted, or are separate. Can you sense that longing for connection within you? Is there a part of you that knows the universality of that longing? Can you recognize the humanness of that desire? And don't worry if you can't—we have this entire book to explore that together. We (re)discover belonging by longing for it. We long for it because we feel we've lost it. To *be longing* requires opening to all the ways we feel we don't belong. You do not need to be a nerdy Black immigrant spiritual womanist weirdo cancer survivor with a unique name to feel you don't belong (though it helps). All of us are taught to not belong. We feel we don't belong and presto, our survival instinct triggers our longing to belong. This profound longing may be the only thing that can save us from extinction.

If we don't feel belonging, it turns out we can *learn* to feel it because it's wired into us. Through evolution, our common ancestors developed this innate sense of connection in order to survive. Without claws and fangs, our only choice was to band together. Human beings are expertly adapted for connection and cooperation. "Disaster myths" is the term coined to describe the opposite: it's a falsehood that people will act irrationally and selfishly when tragedy strikes. In dire circumstances, we instinctively default to belonging without distinction, rallying to help complete strangers. The recent demonstrations of local and global compassion in response to the COVID-19 pandemic are only one example. Kindness and generosity are encoded within each one of us. And when we feel belonging, we are able to meet people, situations, difficulties, joys . . . *life* with more kindness, generosity, and ease.

Throughout this book, I will use many words in my attempt to explain a simple paradox: *Although we are not one, we are not separate. And although we are not separate, we are not the same.* Human survival depends on understanding this truth. At the heart of not belonging is what I refer to as "the delusion of separation"—the belief that you are separate from other people, from other beings, and from nature itself. And it *is* a delusion. You are not separate. You never were. You never will be. Yes, you have a body and a history. You have a unique biography that makes you who you are as an individual—including all of your anxieties and all of your identities. You have trauma—we all do. There is oppression and injustice, and particular communities are targeted and terrorized. And certain people continually cultivate hatred and division. There are differences between you and that person or people to whom you feel you do not belong. That still doesn't make you separate from them or anything else.

Confused? That's the nature of paradox. There are paradoxes. Get used to it!

1

The Delusion of Separation

We Were Never Separate

Two Truths, Two Surgeons

Caitlin and I sat at one end of the dining room table as her mom stood in the doorway to the kitchen holding a list of words and their definitions. Quizzing us for our upcoming grammar test, Mrs. O'Toole read each definition and we identified the word and spelled it aloud. Both of us were stumped. We simply could not remember what word meant "two surgeons hanging out." We gave up. Then her mom said: "It's a pair a' docs." My mind was blown. I thought it was the cleverest thing I'd ever heard (at ten years old).

Maybe being an immigrant has made it easier for me to accept the paradoxes of belonging. Immigrant children are not only linguistically bilingual, they are fluent in different ways of being. I lived in two very different worlds and learned the ways of both of them. At home, there was one language, food, and set of customs. Outside of my home there were different versions of these things. Not just actual language, but ways of interacting, moving the body, and being itself differed, as did priorities and preoccupations. I knew that the other fathers did not disappear for years to fight in a guerilla army focused on self-determination and nationhood. Or, upon returning, take their children to fluorescently lit community rooms where unbearably long speeches were delivered for the Eritrean People's Liberation Front. I came home from my dad's rallies and like a tiny African dictator, gathered the neighborhood white boys together. Fists raised in the air, I marched them in the mud around the dogwood tree outside our front door as we chanted "Long live E.P.L.F.! Long live E.P.L.F!" Besides my family, there wasn't much blackness around me, especially where I lived and played day to day. I studied American childhood, mastering the language of prime-time television, Top 40 radio, Star Wars action figures, and Shel Silverstein poetry. I explained to my mom that, no, it was not okay to serve duck at Thanksgiving, and yes, we really did need costumes for Halloween. Sometimes, I was not capable of being the child ambassador because the seventies were too close to 1964 and DC was just south enough of the Mason-Dixon. When my brother's friend Jimmy called him a nigger, Asgede punched him in the nose. When Buzzy from down the street dressed like a Klansman for Halloween, we all kept our mouths shut.

Because my parents did not immerse us in our immigrant culture, I didn't have a real introduction to Black culture until my late teens. By the time I reached adolescence, my cultural references were already formed, and they were largely those of the dominant white mainstream. I may have been the only Black person at the Depeche Mode concert at Merriweather Post Pavilion in 1987. In high school and college, race/racism (inextricably intertwined as we will explore later) became the focus of much of my intellectual explorations, but I still mostly associated with white people. I felt awkward and out of place with most Black folks because I had internalized oppression after years of what Pastor Michael McBride calls "reaching for whiteness." But after constantly encountering ignorance and bias in the largely white social situations where I was often "the only one," I grew to resent white people.

I belonged to all of this.

I have explored spiritual philosophies since my teens and practiced meditation in Buddhist traditions since my early twenties. I have been engaged in social justice work professionally since around the same time. I have also been Black and female my entire life. How do you acknowledge differences and inequities yet also hold a firm conviction that fundamentally we are all irrevocably interconnected and belong to each other? In some schools of Buddhism, this paradox is called the "Doctrine of Two Truths"—the absolute or ultimate truth of interconnection and the relative or conventional truth of difference. The absolute and relative seem to contradict each other (that's why it's a paradox!) but they describe only one reality. Belonging flourishes within this paradox: *everything is connected, yet everything is experienced as separate.*

I felt separate and resented white people—my relative truth. What I didn't yet understand was my deep interconnection with them, everyone and everything—the absolute truth. Science and ancient wisdom traditions both tell us that everything is absolutely enmeshed. Our own senses reveal that there are relative differences between things. Absolute truth is the true nature of the relative—there is unity underlying all distinctions. Relative truth is the manifestation of the absolute—we experience the world through our disparate circumstances. Denying either side of this paradox leads to not belonging. Our collective freedom depends on us remembering that we belong to everything and allowing others to do the same.

Nothing Is Separate

According to physicist Alan Lightman, fourteen billion years ago, everything in our known universe (all the space, matter, and energy) was contained in a volume one "million billion billion times smaller than a single atom." All the cells in your body are made of atoms. Every single atom in your body is traceable to that teeny tiny teensy point.

Every breath you breathe contains an average of ten sextillion atoms (that's a 1 followed by 22 zeroes). There are as many atoms in a single molecule of your DNA as there are stars in a galaxy. Almost all of the mass in an atom is made up from the protons and neutrons in the nucleus. If the nucleus of an atom were the size of a grain of rice, the rest of the atom surrounding it would be the area of a football stadium. If you were to place all the atomic nuclei of your body side by side, they would amount to a speck of dust. I remember first hearing about this from my high school physics teacher, Ken. After learning about the spaciousness of matter, I spent an entire class period moving my finger up and down, tapping the top of my desk hoping I would pass through the space (which was possible although absolutely, ridiculously improbable).

It was over one hundred years ago that Albert Einstein discovered that space and time, distances and duration, are relative; they are dependent on different observers and locations in the universe. Space and time are fundamentally linked into something called "space-time" and your experience of them changes depending on your perspective. The world looks different to me than to you. If I move fast enough, and you and I are moving at different speeds, the observations that I make about space and time will differ from your observations. Einstein proved that matter and energy are also fundamentally interconnected in a unified principle of conservation of mass-energy. Matter can be turned into energy and energy can be turned into matter. He also said that "time is a persistent illusion." This is not new science. We have had over a century to get this. But we can't get it because it's so hard to understand truths that defy our lived experience of time, space, matter, and energy (also, we don't understand the math).

One theory as to why objects appear separate leads back to the matter-energy connection. Perhaps we are not only matter (separate objects), but we (and everything else) are energy vibrating together. As scientists attempt to identify smaller and smaller units of matter, they suspect that there is in fact no final unit (a tiny sub-

sub-sub-sub-sub atom) waiting to be discovered. There is likely a fundamental unity to everything. This *really* means absolutely nothing is separate. And there are still many undiscovered possibilities including theories about multiple dimensions. As physicist and astronomer Marcelo Gleiser put it to me, "we are all vibrating energy patterns, made of the same kinds of atoms and connected to everything else through the history of the universe."

How do you internalize this if you are not a physicist who understands the computations behind these ideas? It is hard to conceptualize that our humongous universe was once the size of basically nothing. We have a perceptual illusion of space and time that is not relative; we experience past, present, and future as linear and uniform. And of course, we know ourselves as individual beings interacting in a world we believe has observable differences. Instead, could we fundamentally be connected to (and therefore impacting) absolutely everything?

Everything came from basically nothing. Time is an illusion. Nothing is separate.

Rocks Are People: Ancient and Modern Metaphors

We have nothing better than metaphors to use for referring to what we do not need metaphors to recognize as unique.

—ARTHUR C. DANTO

A few years ago, I visited Freedom Park in Pretoria, South Africa, with a group of friends from New York. Inspired by Nelson Mandela, the park is dedicated to all those who, over centuries, sacrificed their lives for a free and democratic South Africa. Filled with monuments, art, memorials, and exhibits that invite reflection and engagement, it aspires to be a cleansing, healing, and inspirational experience. The park celebrates the many regions of the country and especially the wisdom of its indigenous people.

Our group of a dozen toured behind the scenes with a friend who worked there. In the museum corridors, we encountered one of her colleagues, a Black South African man who works in the education program. She asked him to say a few words to her American friends. In a dim, cramped, slightly sloping hallway, this young man (let's call him Nelson) delivered an impromptu lecture. Nelson gave an inspirational oratory about South African heritage, past struggles, and hopes for the future. I don't remember all of what he said, but I do remember this: *rocks are people*.

Nelson explained the concept of *ubuntu*. Many people around the world have become familiar with this idea. Archbishop Desmond Tutu speaks of it often. *Ubuntu* is a Bantu word often translated as "I am because you are" and is said to refer to the humanist philosophy underlying traditional South African wisdom. That day, I learned it goes beyond our species. Nelson said, "*Ubuntu* means that I recognize all people as me." He paused. Perhaps he sensed our limitations. He noted with delight: "Oh, and, remember, all things are people. Animals are people. Trees are people. The sky is people. Mountains are people. Water is people. Rocks are people."

Over the years, I had heard *ubuntu* referenced many times. In that moment, I realized the profound and radical nature of this teaching. *Ubuntu* recognizes the inherent interconnection of reality.

It respects and honors absolutely everything as fundamentally interdependent. This is the foundation for the generosity, compassion, and harmony central to its insistence that because we are interconnected, we inherently impact everything. *Ubuntu* communicates a profound truth understood by the ancients but only recently acknowledged in modern science. Things appear to be independent and we function in a world of distinction but, ultimately, there is no separation.

In traditional South African society, and in many indigenous cultures, this lack of separation is both an assertion that *being* is fundamentally relational and a metaphysical understanding of matter and energy as interconnected. What we understand as "energy" is often referred to as spirit, soul, or mystery in indigenous wisdom. We must take care with all reality: other humans, nature, and what is unseen. Indigenous wisdom, like modern science, recognizes that every observer affects reality, and also that there are "realities" beyond what we ordinarily observe. I am because you are (rocks and spirits). My every action is connected to you (also rocks and spirits).

So where does this leave us? We are because we belong. Indigenous wisdom and modern science both point to the truth of our belonging. Both insist that we are not separate. If you are not separate from anything, don't you inherently belong? Ancient wisdom traditions say it. Contemporary scientists say it. It doesn't really matter with which you agree, the ancients or the moderns. You belong. If you believe neither? Yup, you still belong.

But do you believe it?

For centuries, Western science has called indigenous wisdom "belief." Ways of knowing that do not use the scientific materialist method of systematic measurement and observable, verifiable data are deemed illogical and unsound. Many indigenous cultures around the world do not use written systems, instead preserving wisdom in ways that scientists perceived as "childlike" or "primitive." Passed down through oral traditions, indigenous knowledge is expressed in song, dance, ceremonies, and other activities that seem like play (which sounds way more fun than math). During colonization, indigenous people were ridiculed and killed for their different ways of knowing. Many cultures and people were wiped out. No one knows how much wisdom was lost. Despite this, there are many ancient ways that have been kept alive against those odds.

Indigenous people of the Pacific Islands have a unique tradition of sailing referred to as "wayfinding." When Europeans colonized these islands, they recognized that people across thousands of miles of open ocean shared heritage. These indigenous people explained to Europeans that, yes, they traversed the thousands of miles between the islands of the South Pacific (and perhaps as far as South America). They did this on their large, open boats (think *Moana*) by connecting deeply to everything around them—to the elements, the animals, the sky, the ocean, and the spirit world. This seemed impossible to the European navigators and scientists. *Clearly the people are primitive. How could they travel all that way without written language, maps, instruments, external navigation tools, large ships, and a Christian God? Why, we ourselves had all those things and still got lost!* The Europeans settled on a theory that these natives must have accidentally drifted thousands of miles between islands (eye roll). It wasn't until the 1970s that Western disbelief was finally publicly discredited and wayfinders were recognized as expert sailors and navigators. But Europeans did not only not believe the wayfinders, they banned them from practicing their culture of wayfinding (though the communities secretly kept it alive). With colonization came epistemicide.

Epistemicide has the same root as epistemology—"knowing." Its suffix is the one we find in the words suicide and genocide— "to kill." Epistemicide is the killing of knowledge. It refers to the wiping out of ancient ways of knowing. There was a rationalist/scientific paradigm within European Enlightenment that spread from the hard sciences to the social sciences and into the humanities. This worldview rendered nonscientific knowledge systems invalid. I believe epistemicide is a primary reason we as moderns have lost our sense of belonging. In the process of modernization, we have come to believe that anything that is not provable through the scientific method must be impossible. We have dismissed ancient ways of knowing because they seem irrational or naive. We have placed our faith only in scientific materialism even though its certainties are continually unraveled. Of course, not everything ancient is unequivocally right or good, and many aspects of modernity have been useful. But as the French philosopher Bruno Latour said: "A modern is someone who believes that others believe."

We, as moderns, believe. We especially believe science. Since Thomas Kuhn's *The Structure of Scientific Revolutions* (which was written over half a century ago), even scientists know that science is highly subjective, culturally and temporally situated, and an ever-evolving story. Yes, I said *story*. It's a complex story, involving lots of formulas and apparatuses and a bazillion designations. It's still only metaphor—words and numbers describing realities that are indescribable (time is an illusion!). It can be a beautiful metaphor (the elegant universe). It can be a useful metaphor (mathematical equations). Sometimes it's a terrible metaphor (anything eugenics). Science today (and for some time now) wields power. And science itself tells us that power makes us less likely to take on the perspectives of other people—it's shown we pay more attention to those we deem powerful. If a scientist says so, it must be true. If a shaman does... not so much. What is known through intuitive (ancient) knowing and unnerves the rational (scientific) mind is often dismissed as unprovable, irrational, or simply wrong. Power is wielded by those who master language and argument as well as access and resources.

All language is metaphor (just different made-up ways of trying to describe reality). Some of it is complex. Some of it is simple (and poetic). All of it is, as the Zen Buddhists say, "fingers pointing at the moon." We can call it a spirit realm or the energy patterns, but we will still have a hard time rationally understanding the myriad things that form the mystery and wonder of belonging.

Curiosity First: Why Question "Woo-Woo"?

Curiosity is an expression of wisdom.
—SAYADAW U TEJANIYA

Many years ago, I was journaling when I noticed that "creative" and "reactive" are the same words. The *C* just moves. I was telling my friend Rebecca about this discovery and she asked, "What does the *C* stand for?" It can stand for many things: consciousness, connection, compassion . . . But I think it must be curiosity. Curiosity (the desire to know and the willingness to learn) is vital for belonging. Belonging manifests as the capacity to meet life with a sense of clarity and ease—to see clearly what's occurring (even if it's new or surprising, we can discern that it's so) and to greet it without contention. The times in my life when I feel a genuine sense of belonging, I am open to whatever is happening. Think about it. When you feel you belong, aren't you more curious than constricted? More engaged than reactive? When you're reactive, you might stuff your emotions, distract yourself, or act out. You dismiss a person, perspective, or whole community. When we are reactive, we meet things for what we think they are. When we belong, we meet things with the curiosity to see how they really are.

Curiosity is a crucial component of lessening our reactivity. Rather than react out of habit, we become interested. But how do you cultivate curiosity if you get pulled into reactions before you even know it? How can you be curious about your unconscious conditioning? How do we meet any moment with creativity instead of reactivity? Easy—we open to our experience. Okay, it's not that easy. But it's possible. Meditation practice is infused with curiosity. It's called "practice" for a reason. Studies show us: a wandering mind is unhappy and reactive. Awareness (aka mindfulness), the capacity to bring our full presence to any moment, is ultimately about learning to relate to our experiences with more kindness and clarity.

With practice, we begin to distinguish clearly between what we think is happening and what's actually occurring and meet everything with kindness. We are used to believing all the thoughts in our mind, even when they bring us misery. By cultivating awareness grounded in compassion and wisdom, meditation helps us identify and unwind our conditioned fear, anxiety, and reactivity. We begin to distinguish thought patterns that perpetuate or intensify feelings of not belonging, and encourage those that emphasize our interconnection in every moment. Awareness is key to remembering the truth of belonging—without it, we are reacting to things based on our conditioned beliefs (be they ancient or modern). We can study all the facts of the universe and learn all the teachings of the ancients, but if we are not open to whatever life brings to us moment to moment, we will be cut off from the belonging that is always present.

It's hard to change habits without practice. We get programmed by our own experiences, by the culture around us, and by our collective, ancestral, and personal histories. Next thing you know, we are relating to ancient cultures and other ways of knowing as "woo-woo." Woo-woo is often used as a pejorative to dismiss ways of knowing that fall outside modernity's scientific materialism. It's a jokey term masking a colonized mindset: if Western science can't prove it, it must be wrong. Well, woo-woo is having a comeback as witnessed in the rise of shamanic healing, breath work, plant medicine, and, yes, meditation. And, look, this book is not about whether we use the term woo-woo or not. I'm inviting you to be curious about what you believe, why you believe it, and how this affects your belonging. But this is not about going backwards. If you are reading this, your belonging is wound up in both woo-woo and science. In fact, I am inviting you to embrace both the ancient and the modern.

Epistemicide is at the heart of colonization, but we cannot decolonize our minds by unknowing modernity. Like it or not, your

belonging is dependent on a reclamation of the dismissed ancient
and a reconciliation with the dominant modern. Our belonging to
each other requires exploring what (and who) has disappeared (and
why). We must talk about cultural appropriation and understand
respectful cultural sharing. We are in an era when sage bundles are
being sold at mainstream clothing stores while wild sage, a plant
considered sacred and vital to the health of the planet, is becoming depleted on the ancestral lands of indigenous Americans who
suffer the highest rates of poverty of any ethnic/racial group. Will
we listen to indigenous people when they tell us that depleting this
and other resources will hasten our ruin—that depleting resources
is not simply about counting carbon particles but also about our
relationship to sacred balance? All of us are born into the legacy of
the past and the actuality of the present. Belonging requires being
curious about both.

Here are some more Cs: crisis, complexity, catastrophe, confusion. Suicide rates are increasing. People are divided. Systems
are failing. The Earth is in an emergency. It may not feel like we
belong to each other. That's because of centuries of separation
and domination encoded into systems. But another C, coronavirus, has shown us how interconnected we are, and also how
unequal. My friend DaRa described it like this: This virus has
allowed us to experience that everyone is in the same ocean
because we experience the same rough waters of potential illness *simultaneously*. But it also reveals that we don't have the same
boats. Usually, strong swells in our shared ocean do not affect us
all at once. But everyone synchronously feels the harsh waves of a
global pandemic. However, some ride out the tumultuous torrents

in comfortable ships (literally yachts!), some have crowded din-
ghies, some barely an inner tube. The structural inequities of our
interconnection are clearly revealed when we have such a powerful shared experience.

Belonging is not about bypassing crises so we feel better within
our individual bubbles. Things are the way they are because of
various causes and conditions. Injustice exists because it has existed in the past. If things had been different, things would have
turned out differently. But hundreds (maybe thousands) of years
of separative thinking have led to the decimation of nature, the
oppression of countless peoples, the destruction of many cultures, and the theft of vital resources. It makes perfect sense we
have a planetary crisis that impacts people unequally. We should
not be surprised, even if we are heartbroken. And many of us are
surprised because we haven't been paying attention. We've been
trapped in our collective and individual crises of not belonging,
not recognizing the answer is belonging to it all. Our challenge is
to navigate *it all*. Together.

For over twenty years, I worked with children, youth, and
families in community-based nonprofits, arts organizations,
and both domestic and international agencies. I observed incredible transformation in individuals, groups, and communities. I
participated in victories and celebrations of people overcoming
hardships. I also witnessed up close devastating poverty, home-
lessness, war, misogyny, anti-blackness, Islamophobia, and violence against LGBTQI people. Working in refugee camps in
my early thirties I saw waves and waves of traumatized people
fleeing indescribable horrors. Inequality and oppression are

propped up by patterns, laws, institutions, systems, and forces that appear unstoppable.

In my late thirties, as my spiritual practice deepened, I began to confront what felt like a discrepancy in the theory of change to which I was dedicating myself. I had an "Are You My Mother?" period where I asked the same question to every Buddhist teacher in class, on retreat, and in private conversation: "I understand how practice can reduce my suffering. I see how it can transform my relationships with others and possibly effect change within them. But how will my spiritual practice change the forces of oppression? They seem so large and overpowering."

The answer I usually received was something like: Systems are made up of people and change begins from within. Greed, hatred, and delusion need to be uprooted inside each of us first for these forces to change.

Yes. And.

Many of these teachers were not talking about these forces. Not explicitly. Greed, hatred, and delusion were spoken about as if they only existed on a personal level, not in relationship to everything else: identities, histories, power, gender, race, abilities, class . . . These forces are within each of us. To change them, we must acknowledge and understand them. The process is similar for any of us but, depending on our life circumstances, it will not be the same. *Although we are not one, we are not separate. And although we are not separate, we are not the same.* Each of us must do the work of belonging, be curious about who we are, where we come from, and what it is we do and don't understand about our own delusions of separation.

Postcolonial *Papanca*:
Beyond Margin and Center

All yogas have only one aim: to save you from
the calamity of separate existence.
—SRI NISARGADATTA MAHARAJ

I want this book to reach a diversity of readers: different genders, races, ethnicities, economic circumstances, cultures, and life experiences. It means each of you is coming to this from a very different understanding of what it means to belong or not belong. You might feel like you do not belong because you are radical and loud in your quiet, complacent family or sensitive among a group of cocky cousins. You might feel you don't belong when you are on a business trip in an almost all-white city where you are the only Black person at all the meetings you attend. You might be a heart-centered peacemaker in a rage-fueled activist community. You might be a person with political or religious beliefs that make you think this book isn't meant for you. If you're like me, when not belonging involves other people (which is where not belonging usually begins and ends—with people), you start complaining or justifying. Thoughts proliferate about how I'm right and they are wrong. Not belonging is fueled by these thoughts, by *papanca*.

Papanca (the *c* sounds like *ch*) is one of my favorite concepts in Pali (the ancient language of early Buddhist writing). Often translated as "mental proliferation," the Buddha purportedly said that *papanca* is the cause of disharmony between people. Other translations are "to spread out," "an obsession," or "a block or impediment." When my thinking is not clear, thoughts spread like wildfire, consume my consciousness, and block anything else. It happens to me most obviously when I am very upset at someone. I lose the thread of ideas and my sentences come out in bursts, obstructing anything calm or clear (being a meditation teacher and a human being at the same time is often humbling).

It's not just when I'm angry or extremely distressed. My mind proliferates anytime I get lost in thought. When thinking runs amok, I can become consumed by nonstop mental chatter and this becomes an impediment to clarity—I am no longer able to bring curiosity or kindness to the moment. When I am not aware of my intentions, thoughts, speech, or actions, when my mind seems to be running itself, I'm in *papanca*. Which could mean going over and over in my mind a conversation that I need to have. It could be worrying about an upcoming medical test (what I like to call scanxiety). *Papanca* can be grave or mundane. Try meditating for thirty minutes and you'll discover what I'm talking about. If not in *that* meditation, then you'll discover *papanca* in another one. Trust me.

I believe we have collective postcolonial *papanca*. Modern life has become a brilliant and baffling mix of phenomena—differing identities, cultures, languages, traditions, perspectives, histories, and experiences. And that's just on my block in Crown Heights, Brooklyn. There are hundreds and hundreds of languages spoken in New York City alone. Never before have humans consumed so much difference or so much data. It's estimated that we take in five times as much information every day as we did in 1986—the equivalent of 174 newspapers a day. But unlike with newspapers, this information is being generated by almost three billion people. Social media is a mirror for society—a reflection of our collective mind and heart.

We witness through our computers and phones a stream of human thoughts and emotions—thoughtful commentary and impulsive snaps, loving tributes and mean-spirited takedowns, LOLcat videos and racist memes. These technologies allow us to connect in incredible ways, and they are intentionally created to be addictive.

There is an almost unbearable complexity to modern life that challenges our clarity about what the heck is really going on. Our contemporary life (and Twitter) is mental proliferation of the most extreme and calamitous nature. Of course, our own personal thinking is unclear. But, there are varying amounts of information taken by each of us depending on where we are situated socially or culturally. If we belong to many identities or communities, we may take in multiple viewpoints and might have a better perspective on the ways our personal or collective *papanca* proliferates and matches (or not) with those of others.

The word "marginalized" is often used to describe those in society who lack resources within dominant structures. The metaphor of "margin and center" refers to how, because of class, gender, race, sexuality, or other factors, some people (on the margins) are restricted from easy access to what is coveted (at the center). If we expand this metaphor and imagine concentric circles, those with the most privilege and access occupy the innermost circle. In our country, this would be cisgendered, straight, rich, white men (with their resources—money, property, education, connections, etc.—gathered inside). The idea is that those at the margins are lacking access and resources by varying degrees depending on their distance from the center, with the most marginalized (and least resourced) occupying the outer circles. The assumption is that those in the center of the circle are better off.

More stuff does not equal belonging (or joy or freedom or love). If we imagine each circle is made up of people who are facing inwards, the closer you are to the center, the less you see (with the innermost circle seeing the least but making most of the official decisions for all the circles). Conversely, if you are in the outermost circles, you have the greatest perspective (but have little power over systemic decisions). Also, the people from the outer circles not only see more, they actually visit the center by traveling the radius from edge to center, from outside in (often because the systems are designed to serve people in the center). Center inhabitants rarely travel to the outer circles. Some start at the margins but are moved to the center through colonization, migration, education, or profession (or, some might say, co-optation and collusion). We are conditioned to believe that proximity to the center is a measure of our belonging (and that conditioning originates from the center itself).

Remember, this is just a metaphor, a simple image to refer to a very complex dynamic. Society is not a neat set of concentric circles. We each belong to variously sized "circles" with their own dynamics of access and resources; the world is a hologram of countless multi-dimensional shapes stacked and intertwined, all interrelated. No metaphor can do justice to the innumerable ways we relate. But metaphor is all we have, and if we are going to make it as a species, we need to be able to see outside our own metaphorical circles—especially if our perspective is limited.

"Margin and center" asks us to consider what we are able to see or not see based on our positions in life. You can reflect on your own circles: Where do you imagine yourself to be? Who different from you is in your circles, and is it because they've traveled out/in or because you've ventured in/out? How are those relationships structured? Is there hierarchy within them? Are you paid or professionalized into the center/margins? There's no shame in any of this—those circles are constructed and maintained by powerful forces and systems beyond our control to dismantle (yet!).

Consider my mother. She was born in Ethiopia in the thirties and raised in a modest family as a city girl in Addis Ababa. She lived through the Italian occupation during World War II. My great uncle hid her and her extended family in caves in the countryside when Italian fascists terrorized the capital. She grew up idolizing Audrey Hepburn and deeply connected to her Orthodox faith. After secretarial school she married my father and went on to live in London and Los Angeles, following his academic training and career. On their return, as he rose in the Ethiopian government, she learned the distinction between different Western liquors in order to entertain foreign ambassadors. Upon emigrating to the US, she went on to work for the World Bank for almost thirty years, navigating housing, schools, and a new culture as she raised three children (one disabled) on her own during my dad's long absences. She moved in and out of many communities, connecting with people from different countries and cultures. She made friends from practically every continent, from different classes and professions. Some of her best friends worked service jobs and some were scholars. Belonging to many circles provides opportunities to move beyond the delusion of separation. I learned how to make and keep friends from my mom. She always encouraged my longing to belong.

There's a sociological concept for this called "standpoint theory." It says that marginalized people can provide more objective accounts of the world exactly because they are able to see more perspectives. They have what is called "strong objectivity" compared to those within the center who only connect with dominant culture. Of course, this is almost the opposite of what our society teaches us, that those at the center are objective because they are not swayed by identity interests (but really, they are simply entitled by power and resources . . . and the authority of scientific proof). When we are open, we can learn from the perspectives of those who move in and through circles different than our own.

In my junior year at McGill I was walking in Montreal with my two best friends, Naomi and Peter, a Japanese-Canadian straight woman and a white Anglo-Canadian gay man. This was the early nineties and there had been a number of incidents of neo-Nazi gangs beating up queer people and people of color around the city. A group of white skinheads stood on the corner ahead of us. As we walked toward them, all three of us tensed up, and Peter took off his baseball cap that had a small button on it with intertwined male symbols, a gay pride image. After we passed them, Peter turned to us wide-eyed and declared, "Oh, Jesus. You guys can never take off your hats."

Over the years, the three of us have shared walks, trips, and many conversations about our differing experiences. I've never visited Japan, but I've come to understand many aspects of Japanese culture by knowing Naomi and her family. I have learned so much from Peter and other gay and lesbian friends about the challenge (and bravery) of proudly moving through a world that diminishes your love. Intimate relationships allow us to walk each other's circumferences. We remember how to belong by belonging to each other.

Return of the Sacred:
A Map Key to Belonging

There is a current fascination with ancient ways of knowing. Some of it is obvious and even obnoxious (I'm looking at you, capitalistic appropriation of indigenous cultures). Some of it is barely legal, like the resurgence of plant medicine. Some of it is under the radar, like the phenomenon of Marie Kondo, the organizing expert from Japan. She invites people to acknowledge each soon-to-be-discarded object with caring gratitude, a simple and powerful counter to our disposable materialism. Her simple method of decluttering is imbued with the indigenous Shinto belief in the sacredness of all things. Our longing for the sacred, conscious or unconscious, is a way back to belonging.

Many Western people these days are familiar with meditation largely through the popularization of two forms: mindfulness and TM® or Transcendental Meditation®. Though these meditation systems as well as most yoga classes in the US are taught in a secularized way, they (and all meditation techniques) originate from ancient and sacred traditions. TM® dates back thousands of years to the Vedic tradition of India and Raja Yoga. The modern mindfulness movement is primarily associated with Early Buddhism of Southeast Asia (although all Asian Buddhist traditions have mindfulness at the core of meditation practice).

Modern people have disconnected from the mystical foundations (chanting, ritual, prayer) of these traditions for many reasons. Because results are not measured by external instruments and tools, the religious and cultural origins of these teachings are discounted as mere belief. Many Asian teachers themselves encouraged the secularization or even Americanization of the teachings, recognizing that success in the West depended on them seeming accessible. I also have South Asian friends who would rather study secular forms like Mindfulness-Based Stress Reduction (MBSR) so they don't have to learn about their spiritual heritage from those who often deride or dismiss its sacredness (and don't have to hear Pali and Sanskrit words being butchered by Western people's painful mispronunciations). This problematic decoupling of what seems foreign (and, yes, woo-woo) has benefited the spread of what even science tells us are powerful practices. But what gets left out in the process? And how does it affect our belonging?

The trip to South Africa I mentioned earlier was six weeks. We spent two weeks sightseeing and going to national parks. One entire month was a silent meditation retreat at Dharmagiri Sacred Mountain Retreat Center, the hermitage founded by my Buddhist teachers Thanissara and Kittisaro, a married couple. Thanissara is an Anglo-Irish woman from London. Kittisaro hails from Tennessee—his father was an Ashkenazi Jewish man from New York, his mother was a white Southern Baptist. They settled in South Africa in the mid-nineties after practicing as monastics with the great Thai Forest Buddhist Master Ajahn Chah for over a dozen years (that's how they received these Pali names that they still use). They were also students of Master Hua, a Chinese Chan master. Now lay teachers, they incorporate all the woo-woo in their teachings.

Dharmagiri is not a secular retreat center. It's not even "Buddhism-lite" like many American retreat centers. Our group of mostly Black practitioners from New York and a few (mostly white) South Africans spent the month together doing mindfulness meditation as many people now do on silent meditation retreats all across North America and Europe: sitting and walking, bringing awareness to experience. But we also spent the month chanting, bowing, and doing ceremonies.

Every day our retreat began at 5:30 a.m. with the Chan Buddhist devotional bowing practice to Kuan Yin, the embodiment of compassion. Kuan Yin is what we call an "unseen being." She is considered to be a *bodhisattva*, someone who has already achieved enlightenment, but who returns to the earthly dimension to help others awaken and has committed to doing this until every being achieves freedom. It is said that Kuan Yin hears all the cries of the world. The bowing practice involves a melodic devotional chant paying homage to her and her boundless capacity for compassion and particularly her ability to listen. The chant, a Chinese alliteration of Sanskrit, is *Namo kuan sr yin pu sa* ("I honor the one who receives the sounds of the world"). The room is split in half, and one side bows in silence—heads to the floor, arms stretched out in front of them—while the others stand and chant the verse, their hands in prayer pose. Each verse, we alternate back and forth: the standing group bows and the bowing group stands and chants. This gentle, rhythmic choreography continues for fifteen minutes.

Now, you might be thinking: *What does this have to do with me and my belonging?* I'm with you. Even though I was immersing myself in this practice for an entire month and had been doing this particular morning bowing practice with Thanissara and Kittisaro for almost a decade on various retreats throughout the US (some of which I had started assisting), the Kuan Yin practice still felt uncomfortable. It was like putting on someone else's too-tight clothing and parading around. We were gently, continually encouraged to make this practice our own and find our own interpretation and relationship to Kuan Yin. And as much as I tried to interpret her as a tree, as an Ethiopian icon of Mother Mary, as mother nature herself, even as me—it always felt like someone else's practice. Now, you might be thinking: *Oh, but somehow you came to make it yours?* Nope. Still feels awkward. I've never been able to fully embrace this as *my* practice. This also has to do with my discomfort about taking on a devotional practice from a culture that's not my own (in chapter 6, we will explore cultural appropriation). But I continue to practice. I trust what does resonate despite the awkwardness. I trust Thanissara and Kittisaro and their integrity. And I trust that there are truths that I cannot fully understand—yet.

If it's a vibrational universe, maybe the ancients knew something about the power of chanting. Knowing the depth of my own delusions, I vow to give it respect and participate with sincerity and especially with curiosity for as long as I feel called. Having had glimpses of things mysterious and profound through Kuan Yin teachings, I have committed to deepening my devotional studies and am currently in a training program to explore these teachings in a dedicated community. Through chanting, bowing, practicing in nature, and connecting in community, I have touched into what science and ancient wisdom both tell me—there is definitely more here. If nothing is separate, I belong to one thing as much as anything else. I belong to everything, including things that make me react in suspicion, doubt, or aversion. Even rage.

As I finish writing this book, I am in a cabin in upstate New York. My husband and I have rented it for the month. Our first afternoon here was unseasonably warm for early October. We were lying out on the deck snuggling when a middle-aged white man roared by on his riding mower, cutting the already-trimmed grass on his driveway nearby. Our hosts told us there was a neighbor who complained about Airbnb guests thinking his long, paved driveway was a public country road. Previous visitors had unwittingly strolled on his property. This day he rolled back and forth, creating an incredible racket while peering at us through the thin spread of trees. I interpreted this as a warning. A few times, I tried to wave at him to no response. I started to feel I don't belong, and there's no reason why I should feel I don't belong here. Yet here I am, later that night, worrying that this white rural neighbor is looking into the large beautiful windows of our little cabin. When I let that worry proliferate, I fear for my safety. Maybe all the neighbors around don't want us here, if not because of my race then because of the fact that we are from the city. We can afford Airbnb. This is not a rich town. They see many people from the city, often wealthier than them, using their communities as a vacation playground. We are interlopers on this land.

Then I start to become indignant. I am in a house that we had paid for on Airbnb (where I have only excellent reviews from Superhosts around the world). And whose land is this? I have seen the names of the parks, roads, and businesses in the area (Minnewaska, Mohonk, Mohawk, Mohegan). I consider the violence and terror against indigenous peoples that led to the building of these homes, towns, and communities. My feelings of not belonging lead to reactivity. Over the next few days, I alternately contract (drawing the shades at night, not wanting to play music outside on the deck) and contort (becoming once again enraged and defiant about the mowing man— whom I have not seen again). I spin in the vortex of separation.

One morning, sitting outside, sipping tea, I remember a moment not too long ago after my third and most grave cancer diagnosis when

I sat at the top of a mountain in South Africa not knowing if I would live much longer. Having completed a Kuan Yin ceremony with the group, I felt at one and at peace with absolutely everything. I watched hawks circle, heard baboons shrieking, and felt the sun on my skin. I smelled the fresh wetness of the rocks, still damp from the flash of rain earlier in the day. Rocks are people. I am people.

Here in the Hudson Valley on the land of the Lenape people, a living people with whom I myself have no direct relationship, I lie down on the ground outside. Their ground. All ground. I look up at the sky, the same sky from South Africa. I watch the trees, the clouds, the spinny falling leaves. I see birds. Smaller birds fly low, scattered below the blue above. In the far distance, near the thin spread of clouds, geese are forming a perfect V. As I turn my head and track them across the sky, they break into a new shape, an elegant curving pattern, also perfect in its imperfect wave. They create a new V formation with a different bird at the head. I wonder how they decide who leads and when. I consider the neighbor and know he is part of all of this too. We are, right now, both of us breathing the same air as the baboons.

This book is not a prescription. It's not even a map. It's more like a map key. Does anyone even know what that means anymore? For anyone who doesn't know or can't remember: *there used to be paper maps*. Those maps had *keys*: a section that showed relative distances and denotations of formations, land, water, roads, and anything you might encounter. Keys give you the information you need to make sense of a map. This book is like a wordy key. You need to make your own map to decipher the keys around and within you. I can't make your map for you. But I can join you on the way. We belong to each other regardless.

Domination

Fueling the Fire of Not Belonging

Separation Begets Domination: Letting Go of the Need to Be Right

There are limits to the politics of anger and the currency of resentment.
—GIBRÀN RIVERA

When I was first diagnosed with cancer, George W. Bush was president. I felt constantly enraged by US policies, the ongoing wars in Afghanistan and Iraq, and especially the response to Hurricane Katrina, which highlighted the deep-rooted racism of our society and government. I did not have a computer at home. Phones were not smart. I did not get news alerts in my inbox. Social media was not yet a thing. Yet, I read the paper every morning, consumed *The Nation* every week, and experienced anger and upset all the time. I attended protests and donated money but felt ineffective and filled with negativity. Much of my ire was directed at the president. I had an outsized rage toward him, his statements, his policies, and his existence. I did not want to carry these feelings while trying to heal my body; I also did not want to ignore what was happening in the world.

One weekend, I attended a people of color meditation group and talked about the anger I had toward the president. Someone suggested doing *metta* practice for him. *Metta* is often translated as "loving-kindness." It is the capacity for love, kindness, and care that always accompanies awareness. When we are aware (don't worry, we will explore what this means throughout this book), a deep sense of caring also arises. One way *metta* can be practiced and cultivated is by directing loving energy toward oneself and others. In the formal practice, there are categories of people that include ourselves, strangers, those we love, as well as those we find difficult to love. George W. Bush fell into the last.

Wisdom teachings everywhere acknowledge the benefits to oneself in cultivating good will and the dangers of allowing ill will to fester within. As Nelson Mandela said, "Resentment is like drinking poison and then hoping it will kill your enemies." All great spiritual traditions mention kindness and forgiveness toward all beings. "All beings" includes our adversaries. You are also "all beings." Formal *metta* practice always starts with self-*metta*. As part of my cancer self-care, I had been doing *metta* only for myself for many months already. Also, I recognized that there was grief at the root of my rage at the president, and I had been tending to that as well. Often, when we feel upset about something it's because we care about it: our anger and rage are signs of our deep concern and grief. We can also feel anger if we don't feel seen, appreciated, or loved. Normally, I would not tell someone to do *metta* for others before they had tended to themselves, particularly where there's anger or resentment. I was in touch with the sadness at the core of my detestation and was tending to it—I was ready to expand my care.

At that point, I had been studying Buddhism for over a decade, investigating its teachings of non-separation and interconnectedness. I directly experienced moments of oneness that dissolved illusory barriers. I understood that love is at the core of all existence. Over the years, I had worked with a go-to list of "difficult people" (one of the categories toward whom we direct loving-kindness) knowing that on a fundamental level I was intimately connected to absolutely everyone. I knew (like it or not) I was not separate from George W. Bush and all the Bushes, and all the people like the Bushes. President Bush was still a stretch.

Often, *metta* is practiced by repeating phrases of well-wishing (*may you be happy, may you be peaceful, may you be well, may you be free*) over and over toward oneself and others. I wanted to try doing *metta* for the president but I did not feel those phrases would feel genuine. I needed a practice that would really connect me to him, so I made up my own. Every morning, at the end of my regular sitting period, I imagined what it would be like to be George W. Bush. I started in the womb and pieced together the trajectory of his life from what I knew. I imagined growing up in the family he did, attending the schools he did, and inhabiting the social realties he did. For ten minutes almost every day for weeks, I practiced not being separate from George W. Bush, being in the story of his life from conception to present day. I contemplated with kindness and curiosity what it was to exist as him. I considered how it would be to have the same experiences, knowing rationally that if I did, I would be him. If I lived his life, I would think the same thoughts, make the same decisions, be that same person. Then one morning, it came to me: *Oh, I would* be *George W. Bush*. Suddenly, I did not know this only on a mental level. This came to me as an insight: not as a thought, but as a deep knowing. I really understood that I belong to him, too. If I think any differently, I am in the delusion of separation. When I don't understand this, I am in the dynamic of domination.

Separation begets domination. In feeling separate from someone, especially someone with whom I disagree, there's a lack of care or connection to their experience. That separation can lead to the arrogance of assuming I do not belong to them and even that I am somehow better than them. Before my George W. Bush *metta* practice, I knew conceptually that someone's circumstances make them who they are. Yet, underneath there was an assumption that I would somehow be different if I were that person. It's an absurd idea when stated that way, but isn't that what we believe? We think someone with a completely different set of life circumstances, references, and realities, should think, act, and be different than they are; they should be how we want them to be, *and* we assume we would be different if we were them. We become enraged when they can't see things our way. We are frustrated by their inability to change their perspective to what we think is right. This is an *attitude* of domination—a belief of superiority. We even (maybe mostly) do this with people whom we love. Through this practice, rather than insist he be different, when I sensed George W. Bush's life, I felt immense gratitude to have lived mine and not his.

I had a hard time deciding to open this chapter this way. Years ago, when I had this insight, I experienced an all-encompassing sense of relief. When I consider this insight now, I feel a sense of dread in asking others to consider this perspective. *What am I doing?* With all that has happened through history, with all that's going on in the world, do I need to start a conversation about domination by evoking loving-kindness toward someone who is likely guilty of war crimes? Maybe focusing on individuals distracts us from the real problem—systems (practices, laws, institutions) that are used to carry out oppression. Preaching kindness and forgiveness toward a rich retired white guy feels absurd as Black people are killed through state-sanctioned violence, imprisonment, and ongoing terror. I'm talking about feeling non-separation from individuals as children are ripped from their families and placed in filthy cages. I am calling for a connection to the sacred in everyone while people vilify Muslims and bombs are dropped on weddings and markets.

I became so overwhelmed by these considerations, I retreated to the womb-like warmth of a saltwater bath to soothe my unease (there are moments I highly recommend meditating in the bathtub—or simply take a bath). But I would rather feel this unease than succumb to the delusion of not writing this. This discomfort is one of my edges of belonging. And it's where I clearly see the domination at the heart of separation at work in me. It can be confusing to know intellectually I am not separate from others and then slip into a separative consciousness that leads me to belittle or feel superior to them. I would rather continue to explore the discomfort of contending with these paradoxes than defer to the arrogance of domination that assumes I would behave any differently if I were burdened with someone else's deluded life. This does not mean accepting injustice. As I've heard Buddhist teacher Dawa Tarchin Phillips say: *It's about taking a stand, not taking a side.* There's only one side—belonging. It doesn't mean *not* standing up for what is right and just. Belonging includes challenging others and demanding change. But domination is *not* the same as disruption or defense. I aspire to non-harm always, and I can't dictate when a person might need to defend their family or community through resistance. Violence (including death) is a part of life, and sometimes resisting oppression might require aggression. How and when to use force against oppression is not a theme of this book. Knowing that we are not separate from or inherently better than anyone we oppose is.

Years after this presidential insight, I attended a weeklong silent retreat. A *metta* session was offered every afternoon. Each day, I included my ex as my difficult person—as I had done for hundreds of meditations over the years. By then I was happily married, healthy, and in a job I liked. I had no longing for that old relationship. But I still held on to the resentment about all the ways I felt wronged (which were a multitude). During the question period, I decided to ask the teacher, James Baraz, about this.

"I've been doing *metta* for my difficult person for a long time. I have gotten to the point where I truly do wish him well. I want him to be happy. But there's a part of me that's still resentful for all the hurt and pain in that relationship. I keep going over what happened and, well, I feel I was right."

James looked straight at me. He waited a beat then said, "You *are* right."

I breathed a deep sigh. "Thank you."

By constantly ruminating on my experiences with my ex, I was in an obsessive need to be superior. I *was* right. I couldn't let that simply be. By constantly reliving the past, I expended my (precious) energy on my need to be better than. This is adopting and internalizing the dynamic of domination. I get to feel good about my-self for seeing things clearly, for behaving more virtuously, for being separate. Rather than appreciate my capacity for wisdom (and use it to work toward change), I obsess over others—their perspective, speech, and actions. I did not need my ex to be different than reality dictated for him up to that moment. I don't expect George W. Bush (or any politician) to have had a different life. I save my energy for the present moment, for using my wisdom and compassion to take a stand (and address what has been screwed up by people's actions—distinguishing right from wrong, pointing out injustice, making steps to oppose and transform what I long to change).

That person, those people, these groups, systems, and structures would be different if the causes and conditions were other than what they are. Currently, this is the way things are. I do not need to be in contention with reality, wishing for a different past. If I want to change things, I start right now with what is closest to me. I do this knowing the truth of belonging which means I continually root out the ways I feel separate, the ways I dominate others. If we succumb to the delusion of separation, we will repeat the same mistakes. To transform these delusions, we need to understand how each one of us got here. We got here through these bodies.

Not Belonging as an Embodied Habit

Some years ago, I was visiting Ethiopia with my husband. We took a six-day road trip with my mom and sister to the historic cities of Lalibela and Gondar: hours of driving in highlands dotted with small rural farming communities, thatched roof houses in the distance. Often children would line the roads to sell fruit or simply to wave at passing cars. Sometimes we saw no one. As we drove past one village, I looked to one side, and far off a woman gracefully balanced a large bundle of wood on her head as she walked past a man diligently guiding an ox to plow a field of grain. There was no one else in sight. I turned to look at our way ahead. In the distance, I spotted a small figure standing alone just adjacent to the road. That person moved. They shook. I thought they needed help. As we got closer, I could see it was a child dressed in the dark green shorts and lighter green shirt of a school uniform, dancing. A young boy of six or seven thrust his chest in and out. He moved his arms and legs in quick, jerking motions. He stomped his feet and, palms facing the ground, pulsed his hands. We slowed and I opened my window to hear what moved him. There was no music—at least, not discernible to me. Our presence did not deter him. He wasn't paying any attention to us. He danced with determination and jubilance in his own private rhythm.

Not belonging can manifest in different degrees of intensity. It can be momentary or subtle, like feeling slightly out of place at a party where you only know one person. Or it can be tenacious and upsetting, like the ongoing sense of anxiety that exists around our career, relationship status, or bank account balance. Or not belonging can be systemic and profound, like the many layers of oppression that can be internalized (more on that in chapter 5). Regardless of the category, degree, or intensity, not belonging is experienced in our very own bodies.

Although Ethiopia and Eritrea have a rich history of dance (like anywhere in the world), there was hardly any dancing in my family growing up. Neither side of my family danced. My father's father, who was converted to Lutheranism by Norwegian missionaries, discouraged dancing. I remember my mother mentioning that her father, an Ethiopian Orthodox Christian, also believed dancing to be religiously improper, but I don't know why Ababa Menkir punished his children if he caught them dancing. My aunt Hirut was a great dancer, but I didn't even realize this until my early thirties at my brother's wedding. She danced *eskesta* (the powerful shoulder, head, and chest movements of Amhara dance), dazzling us with her grace and fluidity. She must have practiced out of her father's (and our) sight.

Consider the way a baby navigates their own body. There is so much curiosity and exploration both of their own being and the world around them. There is no self-consciousness, let alone thinking about identity, beauty ideals, and social ranking (yet). Babies and small children dance like no one is watching. That changes, and rather quickly. These days some classrooms accommodate different ways of being. It is understood that most kids cannot sit still for hours at a time without fidgeting. Children (the lucky ones, that is) are encouraged to move and engage in ways that support their learning, whether that means standing at their desks or moving around the classroom freely. But many of us remember (or currently witness) the insistence and enforcement of stillness on kids. Children are forced to squash down their urges to stretch or wiggle in order to make them more manageable. Taylorism, the practice of scientific management named after the nineteenth-century management consultant Frederick Taylor, was designed to optimize workflows in factories but has long been known also to have influenced classroom design with the idea that children's bodies needed to be optimized and controlled.

In my early twenties, I worked at an after-school program in San Francisco, and I took a group of five- through ten-year-old children (all Black and brown) to see an international dance performance. I knew we would be sitting still for a long time. Before the show began, I told them that we could spend a few minutes getting our wiggles out. Without making sound (okay, except maybe a few giggles of glee) we shimmied our hips and swung our arms. Their bodies were jubilant and their faces were beaming as they bounced and swayed. I was alarmed when a loud male voice bellowed at us from two rows behind, "Stop that! Why are you kids making a nuisance in here?" Unfortunately, I said nothing. The children disappointedly sat back down and stared straight ahead for the rest of the afternoon.

And it's not only in a classroom or theater that we are told how to behave. As very young kids we quickly learn what we can and cannot do somatically (in our bodies)—that there's a right way to talk, play, think, *be*. We tame our natural physical expression from an early age. We learn to police ourselves. Through our families, communities, and society at large, we absorb messages about what is acceptable and not acceptable in terms of our existence: how to move, how to speak, how to dress, and how to belong or not belong. On top of this, depending on our race, gender, or sexual orientation our bodies can be further policed. *Girls should tone it down. That boy is a sissy. She's too fat. Black people are too loud.* Some bodies eventually become targets of dismissal, ridicule, and violence simply for existing. It's understandable that not belonging to our bodies is learned early.

Growing up, I learned to play sports really well. I was one of the best soccer players in a neighborhood of many soccer players. I was about nine years old and a game was happening in our backyard. A neighbor dad came by with a friend of his to watch us. This friend was a coach for a local league and asked me if I'd be interested in joining his team. I was thrilled and ran up the steps of our back porch to call my mom out from the kitchen. The man stood behind me at the bottom of the stairs while I told her, "Mommy, he said he wants me on his team." My mom glanced down at him. She looked at me, shaking her head. Speaking to me softly yet firmly in Amharic, our Ethiopian language, she said, "No, Sebene, no. Girls don't do that." Saddened, I thought to myself, *I see (white) American girls around me doing that all the time.* The man tried to intervene and explain how talented I was and how happy he would be to have me in the league. My mom was polite but quick with him, making an excuse about time and family commitments.

I assume my mother was simply trying to protect me. She probably retained cultural ideas about what a girl does with her body versus what a boy can do. Maybe she would have responded differently if it was a woman coach. I got the message: playing around in the backyard was okay, but my body was not for serious sports. Even as I got older and she became more lenient, I never joined a sports team (though I longed for it). I learned to contain my body. As I grew into adolescence, boys made comments about my small breasts. As a young teen, I was aware of being observed by grown men. My bodily inhibition became tied to sexuality. This included an inhibition to dance.

Today, many people I know from various backgrounds are not comfortable dancing in front of others, grown people who are otherwise confident, aware, even spiritually grounded. They are scared to move their bodies. Me too. I felt inhibited for years. I did not grow up comfortable dancing or really being in my body in general. I sort of shuffled my feet and moved a bit to the New Wave or Ska music around me. I jumped around to the grunge that emerged in my late adolescence. I used alcohol and other drugs to numb my inhibitions.

I first learned to move my body in gay male clubs in my early twenties. These were spaces where I felt free to express myself without worrying about looking seductive or giving the wrong message to men. I could move my body in exploration and freedom, learning what felt good for me. As I came to love hip-hop and R&B in my midtwenties, I learned to dance everywhere. Now I feel comfortable dancing almost anywhere. Sometimes I even do a little jiggle on the subway platform if a song in my earbuds really moves me. But I can still feel that discomfort arise when I first step onto a dance floor in spaces where I feel insecure or when trying to move to a style of music I don't know.

It's quite amazing when we think about it. Many of us feel self-conscious being in our own skin. We are scared to move our own bodies, the place we have inhabited for our entire existence. That separation started long ago, and I will not delve into why or how that began. Just know three things: 1) Epistemicide (the dismissal of other ways of knowing) affects both the mind and the body. We lose many ways of knowing with the effects of colonization (including dance). 2) When we become separated from the body, we stop belonging to it. 3) We learn not belonging from people who also did not feel belonging (often starting with our own parents). Those Norwegian missionaries were taught to not move their bodies, just like they taught my grandfather and he taught my dad and, consciously or unconsciously, my parents taught me.

Dance is part of every culture. Every traditional community in the world has dance forms related to its music. Dance connects social life and religious ritual. Dance is ordinary and special. In the US, social dance, intended for participation not performance, was preserved through folk, regional, and ethnic forms. There were also mainstream dances (often coopted from people of color) popularized in American society well into the sixties. People danced, everywhere and all the time: in the kitchen, social hall, bar, house party, and cultural center. Of course, people still love to dance, and especially in Black, Latinx, and immigrant communities, dancing never stopped. Today dance classes and dance forms are spreading through teachers, studios, and TikTok. But in dominant culture and for those of us who are distanced from our bodies, we rarely experience spontaneous expressions like that little boy on the side of the road in the highlands of Ethiopia. Not belonging in our bodies disconnects us from belonging. But we still long to belong. That's why we watch videos of people dancing or performing acrobatic feats through sports. We long to belong to our bodies. And we create strategies to meet that longing to belong.

Belonging Strategies:
Semiotic Vigilance and Assimilation

In my twenties I had a boyfriend who was half-Spanish, half-Swiss and went to the American School in Geneva. Alvaro and his brother were equally fluent in Spanish, French, and English. Their best friends from high school, a brother and sister from Mexico City, also grew up in Geneva. When the four of them would get together they would speak in all three languages. They moved back and forth seamlessly, adjusting to the last language spoken, changing—sometimes midsentence—whenever it suited them. I asked Alvaro how or why they shifted which they spoke. He said each language was useful for expressing different things. It felt entirely appropriate to talk about a particular idea in French. Some words in Spanish better articulated a different concept. A conversation about that musician made more sense in English. They had a fluid fluency, effortlessly belonging to all three languages.

Like many people of color, I do what's called "code switching." Sometimes used to refer to multilingual people like Alvaro who flow back and forth between different languages, it also refers to those who use vernaculars, accents, and differing cultural references within one language. My mom and her friends who also immigrated to the US code switched, throwing in English words and phrases when speaking Amharic. African Americans often code switch depending on the other speakers and listeners in a conversation, moving between Black vernacular and Black references versus standard English and references to dominant culture. I have learned to code switch with friends who understand my multitude of references; we travel many circles together. Code switching can be thought of as "fluid fluency." One moves back and forth, in and out without stress. Fluid fluency happens within belonging.

Growing up, I engaged in what I describe as "semiotic vigilance." Semiotics is anything that involves signs and symbols. When combined with vigilance, there's a hyper attention to the things around you that communicate meaning—which is everything. Semiotic vigilance looks like code switching except there is an assumption we don't belong. We move from margins toward the center and back again, all with trepidation. We enter a room and scan it to understand all the signs and symbols of the people and space—its semiotics. We understand that there are many ways of communicating but we speak and move with caution, not trusting that we will be welcomed, seen, heard, or included. At some point in my early adolescence, I became aware that I was repeating everything I said silently to myself. Every. Single. Word. I don't know how long I'd been doing it. I only noticed, and stopped, around the age of twelve. I still remember where I was, in the hall on the second floor of my school, standing next to some lockers when this habit became conscious. I don't remember to whom I was talking or about what. I assume I was checking what I said to make sure it was correct. I was on guard. Vigilant, literally about semiotics. But even after I stopped repeating my sentences, I stayed on guard for other signs and symbols: clothing, music, accent, preferences, references. And, yes, I still do this sometimes. I still experience insecurities and uncertainties about different spaces and places. For those of us who constantly cross borders (metaphorical and geographical), who navigate very different spaces throughout our lives or even within one day, semiotic vigilance can feel necessary. We are vigilant as we move back and forth through different spaces. Vigilance is guarded and stressful. It implies not resting. It does not assume the belonging of fluid fluency, and it takes a toll.

Semiotic vigilance is connected to assimilation. Through vigilance, we observe how access and resources are awarded to those who abandon the margins. We move toward the center, sometimes grudgingly, sometimes unknowingly. We decide (consciously or unconsciously) one group or community or aspect of ourselves is better or more important than another, and we assimilate into that, usually sacrificing a part of ourselves or our connection to others in the process. Assimilation can happen across identities. A woman assimilates to the masculine culture in her office, a femme gay man tones it down in front of his family, an immigrant cuts themself off from their culture, a working-class person abandons their origins for the trappings of wealth.

My friend Michele is Taiwanese American. She once mentioned that her family moved around a lot and went to church growing up. "What denomination?" I asked. "Oh, whichever Protestant one was nearest to our house. My mom believed in God, but, really, she just wanted us to fit into whatever neighborhood we were in." I, too, tried to belong everywhere. But I did not *feel* belonging anywhere. I felt a push-pull living between very different cultures: I never felt like I fit into American society, and I was also disconnected from our homeland. When I was little, my parents called me "Peace Corps" because my Amharic had become so accented (before I lost most of it). As an adult visiting family in Ethiopia for the first time, I understood only a fraction of what was being said. I felt out of place because of my American ways and my natural afro (twenty-five years ago, natural hair was not a thing like it is now). I desired to connect with cousins and family friends from childhood, but there was a distance created by our cultural differences.

When we assimilate in hope of belonging, we reject parts of ourselves that seemingly make us different (we may stop listening to Top 40 hits in public or forcibly change our accent). "White" families in America are assimilated people who originate from specific cultures in Europe. As the study of whiteness has shown, various European people sacrificed their cultural differences (including dance) in order to belong to whiteness (and wealth), sometimes forcibly erasing their distinctions: changing their Jewish-sounding name, abandoning ethnic distinctions like clothing, or refusing to let children speak their native language such as Italian or Greek. Often food is the one way people hold on to their origins—lucky for all of us who experience other cultures through immigrant cuisine.

In the process of assimilation, white people consciously or unconsciously collude with a dominant agenda to keep indigenous people, Black people, and other people of color (who cannot blend into whiteness) separate, under-resourced, and targeted. Some people of color also try to assimilate, even going as far as passing as white. Assimilation is generally a way to cope, to not become a target, or to get access to resources. Through assimilation, the margins are abandoned for the center. Sometimes assimilation is familiar and seems easier. But, again, assimilation requires semiotic vigilance, knowing what is appropriate and what is not. Sometimes assimilation means losing a connection to those who do not assimilate; often it means struggling to belong anywhere. And what if we choose not to or don't need to assimilate, does that mean we are free from feelings of not belonging? Not necessarily. We are still caught in the semiotic vigilance of comparison and competition.

Compare and Compete

It is possible to belong in any moment, in any circumstance. Yet, most of us have a hard time belonging even when things are seemingly going well. We have internalized the drive to compare and compete so that it is continuous and largely unconscious. As kids, we internalize the messages of our parents, teachers, peers and the culture around us and distort our natural way of being. As it is said, it's like we have become human *doings* instead of human *beings*. And each of us learns what is acceptable to do in our body by watching those around us. We learn to compare ourselves, and we learn to compete. By the time we are grown-ups (or even adolescents), we hustle relentlessly to "be better"—smarter, healthier, cooler, thinner, richer, funnier, prettier, calmer, and woker. The "-er" at the end of these words is *comparison and competition*.

I am generally fit. But after years of various treatments for cancer (not to mention aging—it happens), my body is a lot less strong than it once was. From time to time, I sense a very judgemental "I need to be *fitter*" comparison arising in me. I am comparing myself with my past fitness, with others my age, and (ridiculously) with the young people around me. I want to take care of myself, but this is not self-care. It is based in anxiety and distress, not care and compassion. Perhaps you recognize an "-er" (or a few) within yourself? It's often an unceasing contest with yourself or others. And few of us are immune.

Take a now-ubiquitous space, the yoga class. For most of us, it is almost impossible not to start the process of comparing from the moment we enter the room. We look at other people's bodies, their clothes, their hair, their tattoos. We evaluate who we think they are in relation to us. *Is this woman like me or is she different? Is that a wedding band? Is that person wearing Lululemon? I hate (or maybe love) Lululemon. Is that woman into me? I hate white yoga people. Is that guy gay? Wow, she's really gorgeous.* We look around and without deliberately doing so are considering who is cuter, thinner, cooler, stronger, trendier. And class hasn't even started yet! When we start moving, we evaluate who is better at certain poses and maybe feel envy or glory depending on how we think we are doing compared to the person next to us. And you don't need to do yoga to know what I'm talking about: maybe it's a café or the gym. Or maybe you're looking to see what people are reading on the subway and judging their choices. Perhaps you find yourself noticing what kind of car your neighbors drive and suddenly have the desire for a fancier ride (or disdain for theirs). We are driven to compare and compete. Comparison and competition are the primary fuel for separation, domination, and not belonging. And this starts young.

Not belonging is a cumulative condition. It stems from all the tiny moments of comparing ourselves and competing with others. We learn these habits in childhood and eventually they become incessant and largely unconscious. Almost all of us are trapped in cycles of comparison and competition—of course we are. From the time we are able to move, we are rated on our performance. Even parents who try their best not to pressure children into striving and succeeding can't help practically peeing themselves when their kid achieves something, often anything (eating, walking, talking). We come into the world and almost immediately there's assessment and evaluation:

She is so alert for an infant.

They were walking at ten months.

He could speak in complete sentences at two.

She got in everywhere she applied.

They're the fastest/smartest/most-bestest in their class/ group/universe.

We learn that appreciation, acceptance, and sometimes even love are connected to how we measure up. How could this not affect our sense of belonging? Certain views, speech, or actions gain us more approval than others, whether that is in our families, friend groups, or in society writ large:

I get attention when I act goofy.

When I get good grades, Mommy and Daddy are happy.

It makes the cool kids laugh when I make snide remarks about others.

When my naturally curly hair is straightened, I get more looks from certain people.

Even when we are not consciously comparing or in competition, we may be *feeling* compared and in competition. There's a story my mother used to tell over and over about how I distinguished formal and familiar verbal conjugation from the time I started to speak Amharic. I'm told that I would use the familiar conjugation when talking *to* my parents, yet when talking to strangers *about* my parents, I would switch to formal conjugation. This story was a point of pride for me when I was little because it made me feel good about myself and reinforced the family idea that I was smart. It helped me feel a sense of belonging because I was never labeled as smart in elementary school (I got *very* bad grades). Smart was "good," so being smart somewhere (anywhere) made me feel like I belonged.

I was talking to my brother some years ago. Maybe I was needing to feel good about myself because I mentioned this family story. He snapped at me, "You always have to show that you're the smart one." I immediately shut up. When I reflected on it later I realized that, unlike me, he had *really* struggled in school. While I was troubled and underperforming only in elementary school, he had an undiagnosed learning disability all throughout his formal education. In immigrant families, where academic achievement is often prized as the primary way to measure arrival and success in a new life (and anxieties about scholastic performance can lead to mental health issues in kids), his feeling of not belonging was triggered every time my mom told this seemingly trivial story. She probably loved telling the story because it made her proud to have a smart daughter. She didn't tell it to spite my brother; she told it because it made her feel a sense of belonging as an immigrant mom among a bunch of other immigrant moms comparing their high-achieving kids.

All this comparison (conscious or unconscious, minor or significant) leads us into separation and domination—into competitive feelings of doubt, deficiency, and despair. This is because when we compare ourselves to others (or are being compared), we are engaged in near-constant self-judgements and critiques. Actually, in contemporary culture, we are comparing ourselves so much that we are usually unconscious of how we incessantly categorize other individuals in relation to ourselves based on supposed differences in intelligence, attractiveness, athleticism, success, or other factors.

Think about it: if you are in a public place (public space includes social media) and observing people, are you not "reading" everyone around you? It might not even be negative: you are simply taking in all the data about someone based on their perceived gender, race/ethnicity, class, accent, size, or other "social location." You look at their clothes, accessories, vehicles, and contents of their shopping cart. If it's online, you examine their follower count, posts, and likes. Then all of this information is processed through past experiences of similar people. You then make an evaluation of who they are and also who they are in relation to you: *Are they popular? Are they woke? Is she prettier? Are they racist? Is he successful? Are they smarter? Is that someone I would hang out with? Is that post funny? Is it sexist? Am I attracted to them?* Typically, we measure on some socially subscribed scale, but we are indeed *measuring*. This puts everything into the dynamic of domination.

Greater Than, Less Than, and Equal To: *Mana* and the Dominance of Comparing Mind

Often, when I'm in contention with life—when I feel separate or that I don't belong—I am participating in domination. When I am trying to justify why I am right about something or in shame about something I have said, I believe the delusion of separation or doubt my belonging. Either way, I am in the dynamic of dominance, comparing who or what is better or worse.

In Buddhist teaching this process of comparison and competition is called *mana*, which literally means "to measure." It is sometimes referred to as "comparing mind" and is directly linked to not belonging. It is part of our biological makeup to see difference, to compare or *measure*. This is a human developmental process. As babies, we have a period where we recognize that we are everything and everything is us. Eventually, babies develop language, perception, and the capacity to distinguish objects. That is how we learn to navigate the world and other people. Though nothing is energetically separate, it's necessary to distinguish objects. Our mind allows us to see difference for this reason.

Not only is seeing difference normal, in our increasingly multicultural world, difference should be celebrated. If we decide *not to see difference*, we end up negating people's stories and their lives. We are human. We use language to understand our reality. Language begets stories. And stories are how we make sense of anything. We don't want to get stuck in our stories, but we do want to understand different histories. As the late Black lesbian poet and essayist Audre Lorde said, difference has a *creative function* in our lives. "Celebrate diversity" is not just an empty slogan: it points to the connection and belonging that hearing each other's stories creates. We can understand our current crisis of not belonging by exploring what got each of us here. As Lorde says, "Difference is that raw and powerful connection from which our personal power is forged." I can tell you what it was like growing up Black, an immigrant, and a girl, and that helps you relate to your own sense of belonging regardless of your background or history.

Comparing becomes problematic when it is not grounded in a fundamental understanding of belonging. When comparison is rooted in separation, it becomes competitive. This is what the teaching on *mana* is telling us. *Mana* has three possible expressions—we compare things as greater than, less than, or equal to. We are caught within a dynamic of domination whether we think we are better, worse, or the same. Isn't that last one interesting? Being the same is still being separate. For many of us, our ultimate goal is essentially to abandon the categories of *greater than* and *less than* and recognize each other's inherent equality. However, this ancient wisdom teaching is saying, no, that's not far enough, even *equal to* is a problem. The teaching on *mana* says: *Stop measuring yourself against others at all! We are everything. We are individual beings.*

Once again, we encounter the absolute and the relative. Paradoxes, people! Both are always true. Can we recognize separation as a delusion and also honor our differences? Can we recognize both the absolute and the relative? It certainly requires practice. It's said *mana* is one of the last challenges to disappear before full awakening, so, um, get used to it. We might not get there completely. Or, I'll speak for myself—I certainly have not gotten there, except in moments. Moments when there has been a sense of interconnection. Times when the feeling of separateness and the need to dominate have seemingly dissolved. Even if only for one breath, the sense of distinctions and judgements drop away, and there is a feeling of connection and appreciation for everything, all of nature. Even everyone in the yoga class.

The important thing to understand is that comparing mind can become unconscious and exaggerated, and this limits us. When we are constantly (and mindlessly) comparing ourselves, we are limiting our capacity to truly belong to everyone and everything. Let's assume *mana* (comparing mind) is around until the very end (because it will be): let's work with it skillfully. We can learn to see it, engage with it critically, maybe even lessen its most egregious expressions. And we can each begin by understanding how comparing mind formed within us and how it continues to operate.

Compare and Despair:
Systemic *Mana*

"Compare and despair" is a saying for a reason.

I had one coaching client, Ana, a beautiful and brilliant scientist in her midthirties, who unrelentingly appraised her success, never believing it was enough. Tall and thin with black bangs that frame deep brown eyes, she looks directly at you with a steady and attentive gaze. When I first met her, she told me she graduated from the best schools, had worked at the top of her highly competitive field in interesting jobs around the world, had a wonderful partner, and always felt that she was not enough. "Anytime I walk into a room, something in me knows that I can find someone there who is more accomplished, more talented, thinner, prettier, nicer, or smarter. I feel like I am still in school, competing to be the best." This incessant comparing made her feel she did not belong no matter how much she succeeded.

Ana is the oldest daughter in a loving working-class family who immigrated to the US from Spain. Growing up, she felt responsible for her younger siblings and she chased success in order to honor her parents' hard work and sacrifice. The family never acknowledged the trauma of living through Franco's Spain and all that they lost (family, culture, connection) in their immigration. They also quickly absorbed the American drive for academic and material success.

Ana was thrust into a highly competitive academic track and career. Society rewarded her for this with achievement and accolades, but this took its toll on her body and mind. Even though she was otherwise extremely healthy, the confluence of family trauma and cultural pressures produced such tension in Ana that she was manifesting physical and emotional symptoms (migraines, low energy, and mood swings).

I encouraged Ana to work with what in popular psychology is called the "inner critic" (more about this in chapter 5). Inner critics develop in us initially as survival strategies, monitoring and pre-scribing ways of behaving that allow us to stay safe, get love, and find well-being. Usually stemming from traumas or challenges in our childhoods, inner critics mean well and may have served some purpose when we were young. For Ana, like many immigrants, her inner critics insisted that she be not only good, they insisted she be the best. As the oldest child and the one most academically gifted, she received messages, often in the form of praise, that she had to be responsible and succeed in order to ensure her family's continued survival. These messages became unconscious patterns. Ana and I worked together to understand these patterns and create practices to change them. The shifts she experienced were central to reclaiming her belonging.

Inner critics and other internalized patterns of comparison and competition inevitably outlast their usefulness and don't support our quest for belonging. In fact, these patterns not only increase our comparing and competitive mind, they are often intertwined with them. It's hard to untangle them because they are so much a part of our modern culture. So much so that they become systemic.

Habits of comparison and competition are dictated by the society around us, in our families, communities, and cultures. And they play out both personally and collectively. We compare ourselves to other individuals and we also compare ourselves to a group, community, or an entire culture. When comparing ourselves to what is around us, whether on the personal or collective level, the sense of not belonging can arise simply because we perceive ourselves as different from what is labeled "the norm." "Systemic *mana*" is what I'm thinking of as the cultural and collective expression of comparison and competition that is expressed through societal norms (at its most benign) or hierarchy and oppression (at its most violent). This also often begins when we are young. It certainly did for me.

I was always comparing the two separate cultures I most inhabited: American and Ethiopian/Eritrean. And based on the messages I was getting from the media, my school, and my peers, it was clear that I was supposed to prefer the American culture. Often, we feel different (or worse, are *made* to feel different) than those around us because of our race, gender, sexuality, class, size, etc.—or maybe because our family (or just us) seems somehow weird or out of place. Whether we are the only woman in a conference room, the lone guy into historical fiction among jocks, or the only Black family for blocks (as my family was), difference can create a sense of separation—especially when that difference matches the hierarchies designated by society.

As a child, I learned to make comparisons: between our simple red brick house (which was rented rather than owned and the smallest on the block) and the large spacious homes of our neighbors; between the spicy, pungent stews that my mom cooked—which gave a savory aroma to our house—and the cookies and the pastries baked by the other moms that left a sweet scent in their homes; between our African tapestries and sculptures carved from ebony and the flowered drapes and wooden toy chests of my neighborhood friends. Their homes more closely resembled those of other friends from school or even the homes I saw on TV shows like *The Brady Bunch*. Comparing my family to those around me, it was clear we were different. In my attempt to fit in I sported pastel Izod shirts and Gloria Vanderbilt jeans and struggled to understand all the cultural norms.

Most of us are trapped in cycles of not belonging, in the anxiety that we are not *normal*. Even the blondest, bluest-eyed, straightest kid can feel that he doesn't belong (he likely lost belonging to his ancestral cultures—the cost of whiteness). He compares his clothes, his grades, his dance moves, his whatever-it-is to the expectations he feels weighing on him. He, too, struggles to find belonging. Being *extremely* not normal (not something I wanted to excel at, but I did), I assumed from the media and culture around me that my neighbors were getting it right—and we were not. I was caught in the dynamics of domination. Even when we place ourselves at the bottom (or at the same level), we are buying into separation and domination. Whenever we compare and compete, whenever we think "I don't belong," we are fueling separation. However, that is actually not *your* thought.

The Culture's Thoughts Are F*cked Up!

I love this quote by the great, late Indian spiritual teacher, Krishnamurti. He said (paraphrased by Jane Fonda, because it's the sixties): "You think you're thinking your thoughts. You are not. You are thinking the culture's thoughts." It's such a simple statement, and in those final six words, it removes self-blame. Yes, you compare and compete with those around you. Yes, you think your differences mean you don't belong. All of this was constructed *for* you over many years. Many years of family rivalries and school bullying, years of standardized testing and beauty pageants, years of sports tournaments and fashion trends, years of racial segregation and sexual harassment. Years of boys being called on more than girls in class, of Black kids sent to detention, of women in hijab being judged, of all-white-male corporate offices, of having to choose a binary bathroom (at risk of violence), of feeling you don't belong.

Think about it: I didn't construct the comparisons in my mind. I learned them from what was around me. From the time we are in the womb, we are absorbing all the messages of our culture. From conversations, from the way people look at us, from advertising, from the kids in the schoolyard—word by word, moment by moment. Yes, comparing mind is just a natural part of our human condition and something with which we have to contend. But in our society, comparing mind is on the steroids of our education system, consumerism, the beauty industry, racism (and racial categories themselves), misogyny, homophobia, ableism, fat phobia, and more. These thoughts are not our fault, and we are still responsible for them—for knowing them, understanding them, and eventually letting them go. But we should not blame ourselves for thinking these thoughts. The programming is deep, it's systemic, and it's been going on for a long while.

Letting go of self-blame can take time. Our culture is steeped in oppressive forces. And those forces are powerful. Once we begin to see this, we slowly stop blaming ourselves for the way we continually buy into separation and domination, and for feelings of internalized oppression that we know are there but can't seem to drop. We have to keep reminding ourselves: *These are the culture's thoughts and the culture is really shitty. I adopted these patterns of comparison and competition, of hierarchy and oppression. They are not mine. I absorbed separation and domination the same way I absorbed language.* Only then can we look even more closely at these patterns and how they are playing out today, often unconsciously.

There has been a lot written in recent years about what is called "unconscious" or "implicit bias." Researchers have found ways (some more accurate than others) to measure how we filter our experiences of other people according to the dominant forces of our culture. Studies show that even if we have conscious egalitarian goals, these can be undermined (often tragically) by our deeply rooted implicit tendencies (i.e., the culture's thoughts). The unconscious mind has incredible control over our thoughts, speech, and actions (including almost unnoticeable microresponses we have to other people). And the unconscious mind is shaped by our surroundings. And our "surroundings" is society. And society is deeply separated.

It's pretty easy (if you are breathing) to see from the distribution of power and resources in our country what and who is valued: whiteness, maleness, wealth, formal education, heterosexuality, ableness, thinness. These are the categories that unconscious bias explores. Race has been one of the areas that is most examined. Unconscious bias toward Black people has been thoroughly proven through research, unrelenting police violence, as well as experiences of discrimination that people face on a daily basis in housing, employment, or just barbecuing or birdwatching in the park.

The delusion of separation is at the heart of not belonging. Whether we are sensing the bias of others or whether we become aware of our own implicit bias, it is the separateness inherent in implicit bias that contributes to feelings of not belonging. When we perpetrate implicit bias, we are *othering* people and are in the delusion of separation. When we are the object of implicit bias, we feel othered and are in the delusion of separation. Either way, the delusion wins.

We all witness, experience, and perpetrate unconscious bias in micro and macro ways: Our felt discomfort around someone who does not fall into either side of a constricted gender binary. The silent judgements toward a fat person navigating a space designed for the thin and able-bodied. The extra security check I received in the airport security line.

I was fuming for at least twenty minutes at the Naples airport after I was "randomly" chosen for a pat down. Actually, I was not the only one. The young West African guy, the only other Black person in our line of approximately fifty people, was also patted down. Not that my anger was not valid or not useful (I used it to confront the agent who, not surprisingly, denied any discrimination)—yet, the resulting tension it produced in me outlasted the experience itself and flung me into a spiral of not belonging. After walking away from the agent, I was engulfed in feelings of sadness and rage. The experience made me feel singled out, suspect, and criminal. The message was I did not belong. Rather than rest back into the deep knowing that I have always belonged, the implicit message of the culture (expressed through security personnel) dominated my experience.

I could barely speak to my husband and sister. I went to the airport restroom alone. Hot tears streamed down my face while I sat in the stall waiting for the sensations to dissipate. They did not. The tension and upset only perpetuated the feeling of not belonging. Anxiety and tension persisted in me for another five minutes. But I medi-tated with it, meaning I simply observed and allowed all my feelings and sensations. Eventually, I was able to reconnect to the felt sense that I do belong. Everywhere. Even to the agent. I returned to belonging. That agent probably continues to single out Black people (and maybe Muslims) for extra security protocols. She probably doesn't even realize that she's thinking the culture's thoughts. She is also caught in the delusion of separation and the dynamic of dominance. She probably has not made her map (let alone have a map key). I cannot make her a map and she may never make her own. We, each of us, need our own ways back to our belonging.

Ground Yourself

Gratitude for the Body

If the only prayer you ever said was "Thank you," it would be enough.
—MEISTER ECKHART

Belonging only happens through the body. Where else would it happen?

When I make space to pause from the busyness of my life. When I stand or sit or lie down, even for a few minutes, and allow myself to become still and quiet. When I feel the weight of my body on the floor, chair, or bed and pay attention to sensation. When I listen deeply. This is when I feel the appreciation that is always waiting to be expressed. Even when I am sad or sick or feeling doubt or loneliness, if I connect to awareness, I am thankful for this body.

Belonging starts here. In gratitude for the body.

I wasn't always grateful for my body. It's taken me time and practice to develop an appreciation for it. Over the years, I have spent an incredible number of hours critiquing this place that has been my home my entire existence. *My boobs are too small. I have chicken legs. I hate my scars from childhood falls. I wish the gap between my teeth were in my front tooth—like my mom's. I want my curls a little softer—like my cousins'. I don't like my nose.* All of that predates cancer and the changes of middle age. Now I have graying hair, an aching back, sciatica in my left leg, more scars from surgery, limited lung capacity from radiation, lymphedema (swelling) in my left arm, hot flashes, and a left breast that is misshapen and deformed by cancer treatment. Yet, every morning I awaken to a breathing body that is capable of seeing, hearing, tasting, smelling, feeling, and knowing. I can walk and even run (mind you, not very fast or long). I do not have any major illnesses (hallelujah) and live relatively pain- and problem-free. Some bodies can only do some of those things or contend with chronic or acute challenges. Some do way more than mine. All our bodies breathe and live.

As a meditation teacher, I meet many people who believe there is something wrong with their bodies. All genders, all colors, all sexualities, all abilities, all sizes. Often, we don't appreciate our bodies because we don't feel them. We have ideas about the body, but we don't actually sense our bodies. If we can't sense the body, we can't belong to it.

A human body is one of the most sophisticated organisms on Earth. It started from a single cell and became a highly complex network of embodied consciousness. Mystery permeates our bodies from the smallest atomic unit through to its connection to the origins of existence. We have the capacity to be aware of so much more than the limited ways we have trained our mental awareness. Some years ago, I heard an *On Being* episode on NPR with acoustic biologist Katy Payne. First of all, that is maybe the coolest job title ever. Payne is a trained listener. In the 1960s, she was on the team of biologists that first discovered that humpback whales communicate by sound. More recently she asked for permission to sit in the Seattle Zoo for a week to listen to the elephants. After a few days, she noticed that she was "feeling over and over again a throbbing in the air, a change of pressure in [her] ears that would occur when [she] was near the elephant cages but not when [she] was in other parts of the zoo." She realized that there was a whole other level of communication that was happening below human frequencies, below the pitches of sound that people can hear. She described the air as "thrilling," "shuddering," or "throbbing." Imagine! She was feeling a sound vibration that no one else really paid attention to and that unlocked for Western science a whole other level of communication of elephants. I'm sure indigenous people have been aware of this elephant frequency and whale songs for millennia, but what about us? Us poor disembodied moderns. Stuck in our heads, what are we not paying attention to? What frequencies are we not sensing? And can we meet our lives with our whole bodies? What can we hear when we really listen?

The Call to Embodiment

There is a body.

—THE BUDDHA

There is one thing that, when cultivated and regularly practiced, leads to deep spiritual intention, to peace, to mindfulness and clear comprehension, to vision and knowledge, to a happy life here and now, and to the culmination of wisdom and awakening. And what is that one thing? It is mindfulness centered on the body.

—ALSO THE BUDDHA

If the body is not cultivated, the mind cannot be cultivated.
If the body is cultivated then the mind can be cultivated.

—YUP, THE BUDDHA, AGAIN

Here are four things I know about belonging:

1. **Belonging is.** We cannot do or undo belonging. We belong simply because we are alive.

2. **Belonging is in the present moment.** It does not exist tomorrow or in another location. It is right here, right now—if you choose to open to it.

3. **Belonging is revealed through awareness.** When we cultivate the capacity to know what is happening in any moment (minus our opinion of it), then we can connect to belonging.

4. **Belonging is embodied.** Even our most supernatural spiritual experiences are accessed through our senses. We don't find belonging by thinking about it in our heads. We can only experience belonging in these bodies.

Meditation can help us understand all of this—if you meditate with your body.

If you have never tried mindfulness meditation, the instructions are not complicated: be with your present moment experience without needing to grasp or reject anything and without judging what's happening. If you have meditated before, you know how impossible it can feel. Perhaps you can relate to this; you long to begin a meditation practice, but you are convinced you'd be an instant failure. You don't believe you have the capacity to concentrate. You are too easily distracted, and it seems to be getting worse. You have a hard time reading an entire book (except this one, of course). Or you have tried to start a practice (countless times) but it always ends in frustration: You sit down to meditate. You use an object or anchor to focus on—the breath, or maybe a mantra. You start to practice and for a few breaths, or even a few minutes, you're able to stay with it. But suddenly, maybe many minutes later (often a few seconds), you notice you are lost in thoughts. It happens again and again. Fuck. Why is it that you never seem to feel the sense of peace or calmness that you believe is the goal? Wait, are you allowed to call it a "goal"?

Welcome to meditation!

Now try this: Connect with your body in whatever ways are most prominent in this moment. Can you feel your body right now? I mean really, *really* feel your body? Are you thinking *about* your body or are you *sensing* the body? How do you know? What sensations do you feel? Where? How do they feel? Are they vibrating, pulsing, tingling? Right now, even for a few moments, close your eyes and allow yourself to have a felt sense of the body. Not needing to grasp or reject anything, just sensing. Feel your feet on the floor or your butt in the seat. Do you sense the contact, the pressure? Now, what about the breath? Do you sense it? Where? The nostrils, the belly? Do you feel the sensations of breathing? The air flowing in and out of the nostrils, the belly rising and falling? Is the breath cool or warm, smooth or rough, long or short? Not changing anything, simply rest in the breath. Stay with this for a moment. (Yes, put the book down, close your eyes, and try it right now.)

How does connecting with the body make you feel overall? Grounded, maybe?

Many think meditation centers on the mind. Actually, meditation integrates the body. "Embodied awareness" is a holistic term for what is usually called "mindfulness." The problem with mindfulness is we put the word "mind" right in it. We conflate "mind" with brain, the head, thoughts. We tend to think of the brain as separate from the body (and in need of "connection"). Isn't the brain part of the body? Where exactly are the mind and body disconnected? The skull? The neck? The mind and body are not truly separate. Those are just words we use to describe our experience of thoughts (and emotions) versus the physicality of life. Our consciousness is not limited to the body or mind; it is a knowing that encompasses both of those and much, much more (we will get to that "more" later). "Embodied" denotes that mind and body are fundamentally not separate. "Awareness" is the capacity to know both physical and mental/emotional experiences. Embodied awareness leads us to belonging.

In modern society, because we spend so much of our energy on learning through thinking, we are generally very bad at paying attention to our bodies. Consider the wayfinders from the first chapter. From a very young age, they are taught to sense the water, spending time in tide pools as babies and toddlers simply feeling the waves. They train as children to observe the relationship of the ocean to the sky, stars, sun, and moon; to bring awareness to the ways of the wind and clouds; and to watch the movement of birds and sea life. And as sailors, the wayfinders sit at the front of the ship—still, embodied, grounded. They sense this entire matrix, feeling also what is unseen by the eyes in order to guide the group to its far-off destination. Now, imagine how a young person here would learn about an oceanic journey. Maybe they would start in the library, but most likely they would begin with our ubiquitous information-giver, Google. That could lead to a YouTube instructional video. They might find a local course where classroom time and research materials outweigh time on an actual boat. This could lead to a degree, research grants, and internships where experiential time on the sea would be dominated by instruments, data, and computer interfaces. Obviously, I am exaggerating (sort of). Yes, the primacy of thinking mind has brought us many wonders—every time I see an airplane in the sky I marvel at human ingenuity. It has also disconnected us from our bodies.

You would think that meditators would be better at embodied awareness. Not necessarily. Interoception is the technical term for this capacity to sense the internal state. It is our ability to bring attention to what is going on in our bodies. Research has shown that even experienced meditators overestimate this capacity, and most have the same level of interoception as non-meditators even though many of the meditators assumed they had more (it should be noted these were American, probably mostly white meditators). There is a call to embodiment in Buddhist teachings as evidenced by the quotes above, but we Western meditators have not necessarily heard that invitation to embodiment. Moderns (us) generally have a challenge getting out of their heads. Many of us focus on the mind (thoughts, really) to the exclusion of the body. We are products of a culture that for centuries, maybe millennia, has privileged thinking. We might recognize Descartes's statement, "I think, therefore

I am." Take a moment to really listen to those words. This is a foundational idea of Western philosophy, that mind is separate from physical matter and that thinking defines and creates us.

This primacy of the thinking mind is still everywhere in our culture. We define intelligence by prowess with mental skills (mostly verbal, mathematical, and scientific). This can create intense feelings of not belonging for those of us who are not intellectually oriented. It creates a disconnection from belonging in all of us. As a society, we have very (very) slowly started moving beyond this separation of mind and body and supremacy of mental intelligence. Howard Gardner's theory of multiple intelligences asks us to think differently about what we consider smart—to consider physical abilities, emotional skills, spatial abilities, spiritual capacity, and other talents as "intelligence." But our schools, our professional environments, and so much about our culture still privilege the mind. The body is mostly valued as spectacle (beauty culture, sports, dance) or as an object needing maintenance for the real work of thinking (through gyms, yoga, spas). "Mindfulness" purports to encompass all of experience and lead to liberation, but in reality, it privileges the mind—it puts it first, literally. Interestingly, in Pali, *citta*, a word commonly translated as "mind," actually means "mind-heart." In many Asian languages, mind and heart go together. They are not considered to be separate. But not for us: mind is mind, heart is heart, and body is devalued. Which is why we need embodied awareness.

Describing meditation practice as "embodied awareness" rather than mindfulness helps to reorient us, to experience what Eugene Gendlin called the "felt sense." Gendlin was a philosopher at the

University of Chicago who in the 1950s and '60s did research with Carl Rogers, a student of Carl Jung and the founder of humanistic psychology. Gendlin discovered that therapy clients who had a capacity to move beyond a merely verbal or conceptual understanding of their problems and connect to a bodily experience of what was happening made more and lasting change in their treatment. Even by listening only to the first session, he could predict a client's success. Clients who paused more often (listening to or sensing some totality of their inner experience) and referred to this nonverbal (felt) sense were much more likely to have successful outcomes. What was happening within was often vague and difficult to describe, but they tuned in to their bodies. He developed a method called "Focusing" to teach people how to do this. The method has parallels and synchronicity to the embodied awareness inherent in classical mindfulness practices. It also involves opening to experience with kindness and curiosity. In modern culture, it's not uncommon to be disconnected from this felt sense and we might need some practice in learning how to reconnect. For many people, it can be difficult to know the difference between feeling bodily sensations and simply thinking "about" the body. By many people, I mean me (and perhaps you?).

Aspiration and Acceptance: It's Called "Practice" for a Reason

For many years, my own meditation practice was very theoretical: I read about meditation more than I did it. When I finally began a daily meditation practice in my twenties, it took me years to learn how to connect to actual sensations in the body. When I first started meditating, I developed a refinement of attention at the nostrils—it's a powerful (and popular) place to follow the breath because of the subtlety of sensations there. After some time, I could become still and concentrated, but my attention was fragile. I could not maintain awareness without the quiet of a formal practice period. If there were loud sounds or interruptions, my concentration was disturbed. My awareness was not grounded and not transportable into daily life.

Meditation can help or hinder us in getting out of our heads. For me, following the breath at the nostrils reinforced my head-centeredness (attention: nostrils are in the head). If I wasn't focused on this one point of stillness, I would get swept into stories. At the suggestion of a teacher, I began to follow the breath at the belly. The sensations were less refined. It took some time to learn how to stay with something that was not as easy to focus on. But practicing awareness closer to my seat did make me feel more grounded. I spent more time bringing awareness to my contact with the earth in formal meditation: to my belly in sitting, my back in lying down, or my feet in walking and standing. I learned to connect with a more natural embodied awareness of the felt sense that was available in any moment. I was more grounded, less swept away by thinking, which helped quiet the torrent of habituated thoughts that consistently undermined the truth of belonging.

Many of us could benefit from grounding in the body in our meditations. You will need to understand for yourself the best method of meditation for you (I have some suggestions and you can explore on your own too). What's important here is to distinguish for yourself what it's like to practice meditation grounded in the body and how this is different than mind-centered meditation. Explore for yourself if you have a fragile practice that can be upset by noise, physical movement, or your everyday life.

And if you're new to practice, great! You have the benefit of "beginner's mind." You can ground yourself right away, learn from my insights, and avoid developing my bad habits. You can use embodied awareness to ground yourself throughout your day rather than centering practice around achieving certain mental states of calm in formal meditation. We are not practicing to become good meditators. We are practicing to bring more awareness into our life. Staying connected to the body and the ground anchors us in any moment; we feel a sense of belonging. Right now, see if you can be aware of all that is under your seat, back, or feet. Actually feel into this. Gravity works, and you can sense it. If not, keep practicing—you will. It's always right here.

Sometimes meditation can seem like just another task we are trying to perfect or complete. This leads to an expectation that we are trying to get somewhere . . . else. We approach meditation, spiritual practice, or a book on belonging with the idea that there's something to gain, change, or solve. We believe there is a goal. In answer to the question at the start of this chapter, *Can you call it a goal?* Um, no, not really. Transformation happens in practice not by getting somewhere or gaining something but by recognizing the right here and right now. We can have an aspiration for wisdom, healing, or transformation, but spiritual practice is a process of connecting to what's been here all along: love, joy, freedom. It's a restoration and reclamation of belonging. Our aspiration is rooted in acceptance. Aspiration and acceptance may seem contradictory (those damn paradoxes again): we aspire to belong, and we accept that this is already so. We discover this through the body.

In the Buddhist tradition, we find the formal teaching of mindfulness of the body in a 2nd century CE text called the Satipatthana Sutta. *Sutta* means "discourse" or "teaching" and there are many of them in Buddhism. The Satipatthana Sutta contain the most complete instructions for mindfulness meditation. It's where much of the modern mindfulness movement gets its information because it holds very simple but profound guidelines methodically outlining how to practice, where to place attention, how to place attention. *Satipatthana* is often translated as "Foundations of Mindfulness," with *sati* meaning "mindfulness." Again, being the moderns that we are, we put the word "mind" right at the start. But many scholars have noted multiple meanings and connotations of sati. "Remembering" is my favorite translation. To me it implies the memory of our true nature, which is interconnected. It also connotes reconnecting the various physical parts of ourselves: re-member-ing. And it most poetically describes this process of embodied awareness. Belonging exists right here in this body, in this moment. We put ourselves back together again. We remember our belonging. This is not a doing but an undoing. We may think we learn to belong. In fact, we unlearn not belonging.

Grounding yourself in the body is the primary means of attending to this riddle of aspiration and acceptance. *Remembering* to ground yourself is the challenge. I can approach this as an impossible task that I fail at over and over again, beating myself up for continually getting caught up in thoughts of not belonging; I've done that before. I'll save you the trouble—it doesn't work. Here's another way: right now, as I type these words at this standing desk, I connect to my feet and feel their contact with the floor and underneath that to this land, a hill in Pasadena (territory of the Tongva peoples) in the guestroom of Aaron and Art, friends who have graciously shared their home for a few weeks as I work on this book. I hear a helicopter overhead that has been circling for the better part of an hour. Underneath or between that sound, I hear the birds in the trees. I feel a slight tension in my back and I also feel the pressure underneath my fingertips as I tap out these words. As I look up for a moment, I see the jade plants that cover the ground and the many plants and trees whose names I do not know but whose presence (I first typed "presents") I admire and appreciate. And then I remember to ground myself—back to my feet connecting to the floor and the land beneath. I take a deep breath in and remind myself of belonging to this body and all that is around me, reflecting on the gratitude I feel for the generosity of my friends. And now, excuse me, I'm going to stretch my body for a moment so I can continue to feel my way into belonging.

It can take practice to learn to feel the sensations in the body and stay with the felt sense even as the proliferating mind wants to take over. The body is always in the present moment, here waiting for our awareness to attune to it. Eventually, we begin to understand the difference between thinking about the left foot and sensing the left foot. Try it right now: without moving your left foot, can you feel it? Maybe it's flat on the floor or pressed against something—do you feel that pressure? Rarely are our feet suspended in midair, but even if yours are, can you feel that? Perhaps there is air circulating on the surface of the foot or there may be subtle vibrations or sensations within. You can try this with any parts of or places in the body, *re-member-ing* them. Since this is about *grounding* yourself, you may want to begin with coming back to wherever your body is in contact with the ground, floor, seat, or Earth. Allow gravity to assist you in feeling the pressure and density of your body belonging to this planet.

When we can stay grounded in the body, there is a rooted-ness for us to experience the brightness of belonging. There's a metaphor from the Thai Forest tradition that says practice is like the wax and wick of a candle. The wax provides the steady ground of centeredness, the wick the spark of understanding, and the illuminating light they create together is the love, joy, and freedom of belonging. If you have a lot of wax, but no wick, you will be steady, but you have no understanding. If you have a lot of wick but not much wax, you can have insights, but they won't last beyond brief flickering bursts. Many of us hear about meditation and we understand why it's good for us. It all makes sense, inside our heads. But we don't actually *do* it. We think about it, flickering our understanding, with nothing to sustain the light. We are a culture of wickiness: lots of bright ideas, not much steadiness. Our bodies can provide us the waxiness we are missing. Rather than following every bursting thought, we sense the support of the body. That's why we start with ground-ing ourselves.

Follow the exercises in the appendixes and you will eventually get the hang of feeling the body. But the biggest challenge is not learning how to ground; the hard part is remembering—or not forgetting. This takes practice. There's a saying: *Enlighten-ment is an accident. Meditation makes you accident prone.* Practice remembering—coming back to sensations of the breath and body over and over again—and eventually, you will remember to feel the body when you're walking the dog, sitting at your desk, making love, having a difficult conversation, or any other moment in your life. You feel like you belong nowhere because you've forgotten you belong everywhere. Practice helps you remember how to feel belonging.

Judgements of the Body:
Sensing Belonging Through Embodiment

The mind can pull us into the past or future. The body is always in the present moment—that's why the breath and body are used as primary objects of meditation. As we begin to ground ourselves through embodied awareness, we may encounter some (or many) judgements about the body that pull us back into thought. A few years ago, I worked with Diana, a former ballet dancer. A tall and strong Latinx woman, even as a youth her body did not resemble the petite frames of other female dancers she encountered. This led her to develop an eating disorder as a teenager and now, in her midtwenties, she was still recovering from years of regarding her powerful and beautiful body as a problem. She no longer danced and she felt anxiety that her eating disorder would return. I worked with Diana on noticing how she often referred to her body as an object, as if observing it from the outside (common among many people and especially those gendered female). She spoke about all her problem parts: belly rolls, big thighs, wide shoulders, fat ass, thick arms. As part of her coaching program, she listened to daily guided body scan meditations. In addition, she recorded personal reflections in her journal throughout her day answering three questions: 1) How have you judged yourself? 2) Is there a common theme to your judgements? 3) What do you sense in your body right now?

Through the practice of embodied awareness, Diana began to remember what it's like to belong in her body, to ground herself, to feel sensations from within and connect to the felt sense. Through inquiry and reflection, she saw how her judgements of her body kept her from this birthright of belonging. When she reconnected to belonging in her body, her longing to dance returned. She began taking barre classes and recovered the sense of strength and beauty she first felt in ballet. She brought awareness to discomfort, inevitable when engaging in strenuous physical activity. In moments of true connection, she could find nothing wrong with her body. Only awareness of sensations. It's not that all judgements of herself disappeared, but discomfort and pain (whether emotional or physical) became part of her embodied awareness: awareness of sensations, feelings, vibrations, thoughts. She was grounded.

Diana was not the first person with whom I worked who had negative body issues. The culture's thoughts instill almost all of us with judgements based on exclusionary and impossible body ideals. And those of us who are female-gendered, dark-skinned, gender nonconforming/trans/genderqueer, old, disabled, or fat experience constant messages, suggestions, and even threats or physical harm that demean or degrade our bodies, thus complicating our relationship to belonging. Even when we know this, the damage can still work its way into us. It can be confusing to rationally understand that messages telling me body fat is wrong are harmful and absurd and yet still police and judge my own body for signs of weight gain. We all know that aging is inevitable (if we are lucky enough to get old—the only other option is to get dead), and yet we buy creams and dyes to banish any signs of it. Treating the body as an object to control or fix disconnects us from the belonging of true connection to the senses. When we judge the body as an object, we cannot fully feel the body as an experience.

Obviously, even if we dislike or despise our bodies, we can never truly leave the body. Whether you feel your body or not, whether you love your body or not, no matter how much it changes through intervention, time, or gravity, your body is with you until the end. You may have limited awareness of your embodiment, but you are nevertheless embodied and belong to your body. Bodies that are not able to exhibit strength, bodies that do not fit normative ideas of power and beauty, bodies that are sick, injured, or otherwise limited—these bodies provide the same opportunities for belonging. One body does not have an advantage over another for this. In fact, in my experience, discomfort is often the greatest opportunity for remembering. When everything is going great physically, when there's no pain or discomfort, I tend to ignore my body. But when my sciatica is acting up? That's when I start to remember *there is a body.*

Get (Un)Comfortable

Pain is not a punishment, pleasure is not a reward.
—PEMA CHÖDRÖN

One of the mighty illusions that is constructed in the dailiness of life in our culture is that all pain is a negation of worthiness, that the real chosen people, the real worthy people, are the people that are most free from pain.

—BELL HOOKS

Society leads us to think all pain is a mistake. This leads us into constant contention with reality. Discomfort, dis-ease, illness, aging, limitations, and any and all ailments of the body are part of the deal of embodiment. It's hard to experience belonging in a body that we believe is somehow wrong or faulty. Yet, we can behave as if any unwelcome change in the body is unjust, as Pema Chödrön says, as if "pain is a punishment." Being diagnosed with cancer at such a young age felt like a huge punishment. I could not understand why I—an early (American) adopter of yoga, meditation, and all the woo-woo—got the big C. I must have done something wrong. I *did* smoke in my twenties. And there was all the partying. Oh, and the accompanying drugs. But lots of people did that and they didn't get stage three cancer. Lost in lamentation, I recited, "Why me?" It was only when in the hospital with kidney failure, awaiting news about whether I would undergo a risky surgery (luckily, I did not), that I released that thought.

I was alone in my room, in pain, frustrated. Visiting hours had passed. Smartphones had yet to be invented. I had no friends or apps to distract me. I was ready to press the red button to call a nurse for drugs when I glanced at the front page of the newspaper lying next to my head. There was a photo of a woman in Darfur, probably younger than me at the time. She was emaciated and held in her arms her dying baby whose skeletal face gazed up at their mother as she stared into the lens of the camera. In that moment, I thought, "Why not me?" What made me think I should be free from pain? Almost two million people are diagnosed with cancer in the US every year. Over half a million die, including thousands of children. Comparison led me to evaluate myself in relation to my friends who were healthy, raising families, seemingly not in pain. Pain felt like a punishment. I felt like I did not belong. But I belong to pain too. We all do. Mindfulness invites us to get comfortable with this reality.

As I removed the "oh, woe is me" story about pain, I had an opportunity for embodied awareness. Letting go of my stories, I used my practice to check in to what exactly was happening. I attuned to sensations and felt a stabbing in my abdomen, the same I'd been feeling for weeks. It was not pleasant, *and* it was familiar and tolerable. I acknowledged that if it got worse, I could call someone to help me relieve it. For that I gave thanks. I allowed myself to rest in a place of gratitude. This made space for me to continue feeling the sensations. I followed my breath in the belly; it eased the pain just a little. I rested in that moment. Turning back to the paper, I considered the woman in the picture again and sent a silent prayer for her ease.

Embodied awareness has helped me manage pain better. This is not only true for physical pain. Studies show that social pain—the experience of pain as a result of interpersonal rejection or loss—activates the same regions of the brain as physical pain. Whether the pain is physical or emotional, we process it as pain. But if we can't *feel* the pain, we perpetuate it through our anxiety and worry about it. My experience is supported by research. In a recent *New York Times* article, cardiologist Haider Warraich states: "[H]ow much something hurts can vary depending on factors like your expectations, your mood, and how distracted you are. Just seeing someone else in pain can make you feel worse, too."

There is a growing understanding of the vicious cycle connecting physical pain to mental health. Those with negative mental states have a much higher rate of chronic pain, and chronic pain can lead to anxiety and depression. An interesting side note: most Ohio and Pennsylvania counties that flipped from Obama to Trump in the 2016 election had been wracked by heroin and opioid addiction. Our treatment of pain as purely a physical phenomenon needing pharmaceutical intervention underestimates how much our thoughts affect our pain. This is not to say you can think any pain away or that all pain is imaginary; I believe it is asking us to consider whether we are truly in touch with our pain or not—or how disconnected we are from our sensations. Patterns of pain in the body inevitably overlap with emotional patterns.

When we can better sense our physical pain, we are relieved from the stories about that pain that keep us caught in a cycle of despair. Rather than meet it with denial or dismissal, we connect to the felt sense with kindness and curiosity. Warraich cites studies that show empathy is one of the most important factors in helping to alleviate pain. Patients whose doctors show more empathy have better results with pain management. We can bring that empathy to ourselves by meeting pain with embodied awareness, curious about the sensations. It's not that we long for the pain to continue. We can aspire for a release from pain, but we bring kindness and compassion to whatever is happening. We accept what's there, without contention. Kindness and curiosity, aspiration and acceptance—these are the keys to belonging.

Beyond Liking and Not Liking Pain and Pleasure

Whether the pain is physical or emotional, we long for a release. In our attempt to get away from it, we limit our capacity to feel it, thinking that will protect us. Instead, it limits our capacity to feel *at all*.

We live in a culture that glorifies pleasure without even actually teaching us to feel it. Pleasure becomes a fetish and a status symbol, not an embodied experience. Those in society who experience more material ease and better fit the culture's idea of a pleasurable life (i.e., having more stuff) are deemed better off. But fame, money, and power do not necessarily make you free or joyful. If we were better able to feel the sensations of pleasure and pain, perhaps we would not be desperately grasping for the former and compulsively avoiding the latter, swinging between the emotions of happiness and sadness about the two.

Neuroscientist Lisa Feldman Barrett explains how emotions are made in her book aptly titled *How Emotions Are Made*. She distinguishes between three biological states (pleasant, unpleasant, and arousal). These are physical experiences. Our various interpretations of them constitute our range of emotions (liking, disliking, fear, sadness, happiness). Pleasant, unpleasant, and arousal are states felt somatically by all humans, however there is no similar cross-cultural reality of emotions. What we in America deem "sadness" has no direct equivalent in Tahitian culture. In similar situations where we would feel sad, they feel something more akin to "the kind of fatigue you feel when you have the flu." Barrett believes our emotions are culturally learned habits that we add onto the physical sensations of pleasant, unpleasant, or arousal. She states: "This is partly why mindfulness meditation is so useful to people who have chronic pain—it lets you separate out the physical discomfort from the distress."

You know who else figured this out? The Buddha. One of the central practices in the teaching on mindfulness is around what's called *vedana*. Often translated as "feeling tone," it describes how every experience contains a quality of pleasant, unpleasant, or neutral. Every sensation and thought, every moment in life can be categorized by one of these three qualities. We add emotion on top of these qualities. We tend to like the pleasant and dislike the unpleasant and ignore the neutral—and thereby watch Netflix rather than work on our book, press the red button for drugs we don't necessarily need, or don't notice the color of the sky at sunset.

The past few years I have met one of the most profound spiritual teachers of my life. It's called menopause. When I was forty-five, after my third diagnosis and second time with stage four cancer, I had my ovaries removed as part of my treatment. This thrust me into early and full-blown menopause. When they first started, my hot flashes were at their most intense. In New York City summer heat, I felt like I was set aflame from the inside (extremely unpleasant). I was also more irritable than usual, grumpy, and quick to be reactive. I assumed that this was an overall side effect of the hormonal changes—until one fall morning; I was sitting at the kitchen table drinking tea. My mind was wandering here and there when I noticed some irritation surfacing. An annoyance I had about something my husband did popped into my mind. Having practiced for years with difficult thoughts and emotions, I immediately went to my body to sense into my experience. I brought attention to my belly and I noticed some very subtle tingling. Using embodied awareness, I kept my attention there. It was about thirty seconds later that I realized a hot flash was arising. This is when I made the connection. *Is my irritation being caused by the initial feelings of the hot flash?* I was getting irritated at the very first stirrings of the hot flash, before the heat. By the time the hot flash arrived, I was disgruntled. My husband's actions were simply a habituated place for me to project the irritating sensations that my body felt but that my mind had not yet registered. I had become accustomed to being annoyed by my husband, something I may have learned in my family—I come from a long line of women who were (perhaps rightfully) annoyed by their husbands. That habit inclined me to be annoyed by him when in fact he was not even there, not even doing or not doing something annoying.

I recognized that my thoughts about menopause may have been affecting my experience of it. As my sex drive lessened and my body changed with the drop in hormones, I developed a similar "why me" bitterness that I had had in the early years of cancer. I was disgruntled about having to deal with this experience "before my time." None of my peers were facing menopause yet. My husband would never have to contend with hot flashes. Older women are barely acknowledged in our culture. I could already feel how I was less acknowledged or appreciated in certain spaces, how I would soon become irrelevant. Those old feelings of not belong-

ing were being stirred. Since then, whenever an annoyance, a
difficult emotion, or an upsetting thought arises, I "treat it like
a hot flash." I recognize that there's a chance a true hot flash will
arise (happens more often than not) but that there is likely a physical experience of "unpleasant" that is happening somewhere in
my body and I am projecting my emotions onto it. My emotions
are a habit.

This doesn't mean we have to dismiss all pain, physical or mental.
I am simply inviting us to bring more embodied awareness to
whatever is happening. It can be easy to go into an instinctual
not-liking mode when it feels like someone just turned a furnace
on full blast inside your body. I can try "fixing" my hot flash by
immediately fanning myself or sticking ice cubes down my shirt
(yes, I've done that). I could project onto an emotion or mental
habit. But practice offers the possibility for a different response:
it's an opportunity to practice staying with an unpleasant experience, bringing curiosity and kindness. Instead of immediately
pushing it away, I can notice what it really feels like. I can bring
awareness to the sensation of heat.

With embodied awareness, every time I experience a hot flash,
I drop any story and allow myself to simply feel the heat. When
I do, you know what I notice? Heat. That's all. Heat is hot. I can
even recognize that there are other times when I love being hot,
like at the beach or in the sauna or when I take a hot bath . . .
which I do almost *every damn night*. I enjoy those times of steaming
hot heat. But I control those moments. I can't control when I feel
a hot flash and, ultimately, I don't like change. There is another
core teaching of Buddhism. That change or impermanence is a
fundamental aspect of life. Every single thing in reality is changing

all the time and we have no control over that. It's said if we could truly understand this, even for a moment, we would achieve freedom and lasting happiness. But there's a hitch: we don't like change—not wrinkles, not down times, not loss, and certainly not death. Not menopause either. And now that I admit I cannot control or change my hot flashes, do I suddenly love them? No. It's not like I wish them to arrive or celebrate every one of them. But I can develop a different relationship to them. I don't smother them in my expectations or moods. I give them space, and me too. I allow myself to feel them, and this makes me a lot less miserable about them.

We long to live with more freedom, with joy, with love. This begins in the body. The teachings of mindfulness instruct us to first know what is happening as a felt sense and then to cultivate an attitude of curiosity and kindness toward it. I cannot control my hot flashes, and someone else cannot will away their chronic pain. But I *can* notice when I feel irritated or when I feel heat rising and meet it with openness and acceptance—that's how we find ease. Sometimes it's said like this: *It's not what's happening that matters, it's our relationship to it.* In the beginning of our meditation practice, we may think we need to make something happen, but, in fact, by relating differently, we are practicing belonging.

Practice Belonging by Practicing Ease

Our capacity for embodied awareness can be trained. To do this, we need to practice. Here's what I mean by that: practice, practice, practice. I've emphasized already that at some points you will need to put this book down (not right now) and engage in the body-centered practices in the appendix. These are foundational to your cultivation of belonging. Grounding yourself in the body is fundamental to everything else we explore in this book. Please take your time with this. Belonging only happens through you, through your embodied experience. We can't develop the capacity to be in our bodies by thinking about it.

Formal practice is important for this development. It eliminates the variables to a simple posture (seated, lying down, standing, or walking) and attention to experience in that posture. As we learn to master a simple process of sensing (simple but not easy), we then expand our practice to daily life. Embodied awareness in a formal posture and embodied awareness in daily life are not mutually exclusive practices. They are intertwined and we will explore both of them as opportunities for remembering our belonging.

When we feel belonging, there's an ease that is palpable, like feeling a deep exhale or the release of vigilance. Central to embodied awareness is learning to relax. We cannot relax if we are speeding from one activity to another. I'll say this another way: SLOW THE F@CK DOWN! It's not that we can't have easeful awareness at quicker speeds, but like practicing anything new, we have to try it slowly (or in stillness) before we can speed up. Imagine learning how to play a new song or learning a dance move—you would need to break it down, try it slowly, learn it at a comfortable pace. Slowing down in this culture is not easy. Many of us have experienced that challenge of slowing down while attempting to shelter in place. The momentum involved in constant *doing* is strong. Learning to relax may sound natural, but if we don't know how to do it, we need to practice it.

The word "practice" can make us think there's great effort involved. But belonging to the body does not require strain. We learn
to cultivate embodied awareness with a natural and easeful attention.
When we do this, many things we have ignored get revealed to
us, not by doing something else, but by opening our awareness to
what's already happening inside. Years ago, I realized that I curl
my left foot by turning it outwards so that my weight is resting on
the outer edge. I noticed this while I was washing dishes. I was lost
in thought, mechanically scrubbing and rinsing, when I suddenly
remembered awareness (I was accident prone by then). I brought
attention to my body. In order to ground myself, I directed my
awareness to my feet. That's when I sensed my foot angled underneath itself. I did not make this a problem, I simply noticed it. I
wondered, "Wow, how long have I been doing *this*?"

Meditation practice centered in the body had primed me to recognize what was happening. A practice that emphasizes ease had
prepared me to accept what was happening without stress. We are
not cultivating an awareness of the body in order to add judgement
or tension to what's happening. Or to change it and make it any
different than it is. We are cultivating a relationship of curiosity and
kindness. If belonging is exemplified by acceptance of ourselves,
my crooked foot is not a problem, and it's certainly not a big deal.
Adding reactivity, angst, or judgement only creates stress. What I
did is simply notice and bring curiosity to it. Then I placed my foot
flat on the floor. Over the next few months, I began to notice this
habit more and more. With time it shifted, not because I forced it
to disappear, but because I opened to it.

A twisted foot is a simple and benign physical position. The response
I described is the approach for everything: awareness, curiosity,

kindness . . . ease. The challenge is bringing this attitude to anything that's happening physically, mentally, or emotionally—benign or difficult. That is the work of this book. We don't think our way to belonging; we retrain our awareness to find ease. Even when we are not feeling ease, we can cultivate an attitude of allowing that invites a relationship of ease to whatever is happening. Talking about social movements, Martin Luther King Jr. said, "Peace is not the destination. Peace is the way." The same is true for belonging: Ease is not the destination. Ease is the way.

The Erotic as Power

Ecstasy is what everyone craves—not love or sex, but a hot-blooded, soaring intensity, in which being alive is a joy and a thrill. That enravishment doesn't give meaning to life, and yet without it life seems meaningless.
—DIANE ACKERMAN

Apparently, if you put "erotic" in the title of your presentation, all the Buddhists show up. A few years ago, I gave a talk entitled "The Erotic as Power" and four times as many people came as I expected. I was inspired by the 1978 essay "Uses of the Erotic: The Erotic as Power" by Audre Lorde. This piece has resurfaced in recent years and I recommend you read it yourself. Writer and activist adrienne maree brown dedicated an entire chapter of her book *Pleasure Activism* (Get. It.) to reprinting and brilliantly analyzing the essay. There's also a mesmerizing audio clip on YouTube of Audre Lorde reading it aloud. Lorde's main message is that the erotic is liberatory. When she says "erotic," she is not only talking about the sexual—although it includes that—but about our deepest non-rational knowing. It is rooted in the senses and involves a vital connection to the body. She calls it "the power of our unexpressed or unrecognized feeling" or our "creative energy empowered." It allows us to feel fully and live deeply into our experience. The erotic is embodied awareness with an attention to joy, to savoring every moment—not for stimulation but for liberation. She says:

> For once we begin to feel deeply all the aspects of our lives, we begin to demand from ourselves and from our life-pursuits that they feel in accordance with that joy which we know ourselves to be capable of. Our erotic knowledge empowers us, becomes a lens through which we scrutinize all aspects of our existence, forcing us to evaluate those aspects honestly in terms of their relative meaning within our lives. And this is a grave responsibility, projected from within each of us, not to settle for the convenient, the shoddy, the conventionally expected, nor the merely safe.

When we do not live deeply into our embodied awareness, our lives become about the struggle to keep up. We become trapped in cycles of productivity and performativity. Much as we have been exploring, when we cannot pause or at least slow down the speed of our activities, when we race through life mentally projecting our anxieties and patterning onto experience, pushing away pain and grasping at pleasure—we are unable to bring awareness to what is happening. We don't pause or slow down in our attempt because we think constant activity will bring us safety and security. We are taught that joy comes from this speed—quicker, faster, better. Our belonging is sacrificed to ideas about success rather than the enjoyment of life.

Lorde describes the erotic as touching into a "feminine plane" within each of us. Although she speaks about the sexual degradation of women connected to the devaluing of erotic knowledge, this is not only about gender. It's also not *not* about gender:

> On the one hand, the superficially erotic has been encouraged as a sign of female inferiority; on the other hand, women have been made to suffer and to feel both contemptible and suspect by virtue of its existence.

The erotic is devalued because it's been largely associated with women, but its diminishment affects all of us. As bell hooks says, "patriarchy has no gender." I would add "patriarchy has no winners." One of patriarchy's primary methods is to keep us all (whatever gender) from feeling the erotic. To truly feel our experience with depth and presence, we would have to slow down a *lot* (which would make us less efficient consumers, students, workers, prisoners, soldiers . . .). The erotic is a deep bodily knowing that is diminished in a culture that values the mind over the body, speed over slow. Lorde describes various activities from political work to painting a fence as falling into the erotic because everything can be about the erotic. Yes, painting a fence—it's clearly not only about the sexual.

And it is not *not* about the sexual. To state the very obvious, sex is a powerful force in our lives. Belonging inevitably becomes

entangled in ideas about sex and the erotic. For many years I confused being desired with belonging and having a lot of sex with
the erotic. Lorde describes how the degradation of the erotic in
sex leads to a type of sex that is about the imprisonment of the
male gaze, what she refers to as the pornographic. I remember
in my early thirties, recognizing that I had learned to objectify
myself through sex. I was an object executing sex, not a subject of
my sensual experiences. My connection to my body was tenuous.
Rather than feeling what was happening, I was somewhat outside
my experience watching the performance of sex, evaluating how I
looked to my partner, analyzing whether there was sufficient sat-
isfaction occurring, keeping score as to what had occurred and
needed to occur. Disconnected from embodied awareness, from
the erotic, sex was about comparing and competing with images
and ideas I had absorbed through movies and popular culture. I'm
not saying I never enjoyed sex or always felt disconnected. But I
believed that lots of sex and many orgasms meant I belonged to
some idea about sexual liberation. My pleasure was being tallied,
not felt. I was disconnected from the erotic.

I have also had periods in my life more recently where I also felt
disconnected from the erotic because I wasn't having sex. Americans have less sex than people in any other country. One in three
women reports a lack of interest in sex. More than forty million
Americans in relationships are having no sex at all. I've been one of
those forty million. Cancer scarred and damaged me physically; I
also became distanced from my body because of the emotional and
psychic toll of illness. The physical and mental stress of those years
affected the playfulness and power of the erotic in my life. Having

had insights about my earlier unhealthy patterns around sex and having connected my practice to embodied awareness, I was less interested in a performative sexuality. My spiritual life wasn't connected to sensuality either. The erotic was never addressed in the many retreats, classes, and workshops I attended. In fact, in most Buddhist spaces, the erotic was denied, diminished, dismissed, or distrusted. As I deepened my spiritual practice, I, too, began to diminish the erotic.

It was only rereading Audre Lorde's essay seven years ago that revitalized my aspiration to include the sensual, sexual, and erotic in my spiritual life. Dance has become a big part of that. I started attending a local studio in my neighborhood. The owner, Laci, is an African American woman devoted to bringing fitness particularly to Black women. She invites students to explore dance using a variety of music—Latin, Caribbean, hip-hop, soul, soca. In class, she encourages us to express our sensuality: this means loosening our hips and whining. For those of you whose dance movements are limited, whining is a rhythmic movement of the hips in Caribbean dance. Whining is not the same as twerking, but both originate in African dance forms and both are very erotic in all senses of the word. But Laci recently told me she did not always have facility with whining, twerking, or any sensual movements of her body.

Laci has danced since the time she could walk and trained as a dancer from a young age. She comes from a small town in South Carolina where the local dance studio teacher, as well as her cheerleading coaches, were all white. She was always one of two or three Black girls in her dance or cheer troupes. When she got to college, she wanted to join the main dance team, but she didn't meet the height and weight requirements (geared toward thin, tall white bodies). She happily tried out for and joined the school's Black dance team but initially was put on the alternate squad. The dance captain told her she was an excellent dancer, but her body was stiff. Laci needed to loosen up. In the Black troupe, she witnessed dancers and bodies that moved with more fluidity and ease. She had to connect to her own sensuality. With practice, she did. She met Black people from outside the South and even outside the US. Over the years, Laci traveled throughout Africa and the Caribbean. When she began to choreograph and teach dance, she encouraged the same sensuality she had to learn and watched women grow in joy and freedom through dance.

I may disappoint you by stating that the rest of the book is not an investigation of belonging through dance and the erotic. But embodied awareness rooted in the sensual is central to our understanding of belonging. If we know how we move (or don't move) and what we feel (or can't feel), we will have a better understanding of ourselves. And knowing ourselves is a key to belonging.

Know Yourself

To Study the Self:
Who Are You?

To study the Buddha Way is to study the self. To study the self is to forget the self. To forget the self is to be actualized by myriad things. When actualized by myriad things, your body and mind as well as the bodies and minds of others drop away. No trace of enlightenment remains, and this no-trace continues endlessly.

—DŌGEN

Who is this Dōgen character, and what in the heck is he talking about?

Dōgen was a thirteenth-century Japanese Buddhist priest, writer, poet, philosopher, and founder of the Sōtō school of Zen in Japan. He revolutionized Zen practice and continues to influence modern Buddhism. What is he saying here? A little harder to explain. Let's look at the first sentence.

When he says "the Buddha Way," he means the path to liberation. Except it's not a way or a path. Remember, we aren't going anywhere. Freedom (and belonging) are always right here. *To study the Buddha Way is to study the self.* In order to become liberated, to become free, to truly belong, we must know ourselves. Why? Well any suffering, dis-ease, unhappiness, anxiety, or not belonging that we experience exists within us. It's not like unhappiness happens *out there*, on the other side of the room or down the block. We are unhappy *right in here*. We may be affected by the external (it might be that annoying person on the other side of the room or the nerve-racking noise down the block that is bothering us) but the actual experience of unhappiness is right here, inside. We can go around constantly trying to change the external world, but it's going to be pretty hard to remove all the people or noises we find irritating from the planet. There will be other irritants.

We must know ourselves on the path to belonging. How can we attend to our feelings of not belonging if we don't know how belonging feels? Our moods, emotions, thoughts, our difficulties, fears, tendencies, our happiness, wellness, and joy—they are all experienced within this self, not externally. Belonging is going to be experienced right here too. How do you study that? Bring awareness to it.

Let's look back at my experience with menopause from last chapter. Remember, I was believing my disgruntled thoughts. I realized that hot flashes were related to my overall grumpiness but I had let that grumpiness spin out into unhappiness about aging, self-pity about my situation, and annoyances with my husband. I did not realize my moods were being determined by extremely subtle changes in my body until I paid deep attention. How well do we know and understand our own patterns and moods? Probably not that well if we haven't slowed down or paused to cultivate awareness. Most of us just coast through life being swayed by deeply embedded physical and emotional triggers. How often are we paying such close attention to our physical, emotional, and mental experiences to witness these subtle connections? Probably not that often. Unless we practice.

You may have realized by now that I'm going to keep pitching the practice of embodied awareness. Here's why. Well, first, I'm a meditation teacher. Also, it is the best way to slow things down so that we can know ourselves better: know that we feel we don't belong; understand when, how, and why the feelings of belonging do arise for us; and eventually reconnect to the felt sense of belonging. Again, meditation practice is not about becoming a good meditator. Practice allows us to cultivate an embodied awareness so that we can observe our experience, know what's happening, and reconnect to belonging. In the process we uncover who we are.

Imagine me sitting in front of you right now asking this: *Who are you?* Consider how you would answer. Maybe you would include your biographical history: where you were born, where you are from, your family growing up, the schools you attended, the friends you have, the work you do. You might connect with your physical and social realities: your gender, race, ethnicity, sexual orientation, religion, culture, nationality. Then there are aspects of our personality, patterns, proclivities, ways of being in the world. Perhaps a spiritual or existential sense of yourself would surface: your interconnection with the sacred, with all beings, with the whole of nature. And what if you met that question from an embodied place? A moment-to-moment exploration of who you are right now: sensations, thoughts, feelings—an ever-changing cascade of sensory data and experience.

There's no right answer here. But the question is important. *Who are you?* It is perhaps the central question within this exploration of belonging. Not belonging is rooted in separation and domination, in comparison and competition. Difference is not the problem. We feel we don't belong because society categorizes and ranks everything, leaving us unable to bridge the hierarchical chasms between ourselves and all we deem "not us." We become trapped in thoughts about ourselves, missing the vital experience of being that is always present. Without a deep understanding of who (and really what) we are, how can we build the bridges back to our fundamental interconnection? How do we know ourselves?

You belong to everything. First, you must belong to yourself.

Ways of Knowing Ourselves: Where Are Your People From?

*My past changes every minute according to the
meaning given it now, in this moment.*
—CZESLAW MILOSZ

I have a Scorpio sun, Sagittarius rising, and my moon is in Virgo. I am a 4 on the Enneagram with a 3 wing and the social variant. I am an INFJ on Myers-Briggs. I am a social introvert. I have the Upholder Tendency for motivation. I have an Ambivalent Attachment type. I use tarot cards many mornings and journal about my aspirations and intuitions.

Perhaps most or all of this means nothing to you; maybe it's even freaking you out. It's true, I am a little "extra" when it comes to typology and self-knowledge systems. The point is, there are many ways of understanding ourselves. Personality inventories are one way and have even entered corporate culture (and clickbait online tests). Still, most of us don't know ourselves on a deep level. What's going on inside? Do we have triggers? (The answer is *Yes*.) What do triggers do to our body, emotions, thoughts? What are our patterns? Why do we keep repeating the same ones? Why are we lonely? Confused? What makes us upset? What situations make us happy? What types of people bring out the best in us? The worst? Therapy, books, workshops, self-inquiry . . . there are countless methods for self-knowledge. I have found one of the most important ways of knowing ourselves is knowing from where we came.

Last summer I met an Ethiopian man in the Albuquerque airport. I was standing at the gate waiting to get a seat assignment when he asked me in Amharic if I was Ethiopian. "*Habesha nesh?*" There was a time when it was novel to encounter another *Habesha* (what many diaspora Ethiopians and Eritreans call each other) in the US. Even in current immigrant strongholds like Washington, DC, it was exciting to spot someone, share a look, stop, and exchange information. We constantly sought the bond of belonging. Now with hundreds of thousands of us from coast to coast, even in small cities, it isn't the same response as in the past—you might offer a simple bow of the head or a few words of greeting. I did not think much of this particular interaction—a quick exchange. I was called to the counter and when I finished with the agent, he was gone. I forgot about him until I boarded.

Gebre was absolutely delighted that we were seated next to each other. He repeatedly exclaimed the good fortune of our reunion. It was his first trip to the US. After a monthlong training in remote New Mexico, he was extremely homesick, eager to see his wife and two children. He was overjoyed to be with me for a leg of the journey. He missed Addis Ababa, Ethiopian food, and the warmth of our people. He found Americans to be distant. We talked about everything and nothing. Gebre laughed and laughed at what I call my "baby Amharic." He could not fathom that I had lost our language, that I had lived outside Ethiopia longer than he'd been alive. He kept trying to convince me that I should return to Addis, that Ethiopia is my home. I could open a business or work for an NGO. I smiled and said, "This is my home." With this, he became very serious, "*Ay. Ay. Ay.*" ("No. No. No.") We had been switching back and forth between the two languages. Now he shook his head and spoke only in Amharic, "Don't say that. This is not your home. You are from the earth of our country. That is your land. That land is who you are. Ethiopia is your home. You belong there."

There are over eighty languages spoken in Ethiopia alone, each representing a different ethnicity. I will never understand all the complexities of cultures and experiences that shape where I came from. There is so much I don't know about my origins, my ancestors, my people. I am largely ignorant of the history of Ethiopia and Eritrea, the Horn, or the continent of Africa. Most importantly, I can't communicate. I speak enough Amharic to engage at family gatherings on my mother's side, but I don't speak any Tigrinya, the language of my father's family from Eritrea. Even in Amharic, I cannot follow complex conversations and I am illiterate in its writing system. Do I belong to a place I don't know, don't understand?

When I teach retreats and workshops, I always start with a connecting exercise where people are invited to share in a small group their response to the question: *Where are your people from?* It is a complex question for those who through enslavement, colonization, genocide, migration (forced or voluntary), adoption, and cultural mixing do not have a sense of their people. Although the accessibility of genetic ancestry research is providing more information, few modern people have a deep knowledge of their ancestors.

Regardless what you think you know about them, your ancestors are here. Whether or not you know your lands, cultures, or birth families, your ancestors have shaped you. Your eyes, your smile, the tenor of your voice, the shade of your skin, the contours of your thighs, the length of your gait—all of these physical traits are handed down to you. Epigenetic research reveals that memories and experiences (including traumas) are handed down as well. "Where are your people from?" implies both location and history: what region, environment, circumstances, joys, sorrows, stories, rituals, relationships you are from.

The Native American concept of "seven generations" is usually attributed to an Iroquois law outlining the responsibility for the sustainability of future generations. It instructs that when important decisions are being made, one should consider their impact on seven generations into the future. The idea of considering seven generations can be found in many native cultures. In Ethiopia and Eritrea, it is considered important to be able to count seven generations in both your matrilineal and patrilineal lineages and to know all the relatives in that accounting (and not to intermarry amongst those calculated). Every single person (probably close to one thousand) for seven generations is to be counted. Specific community members are given that task, and it is a sign of greatness to be one of those who can remember all the names.

Why seven? It's at seven generations back that less than 1 percent of your DNA is likely to have come from any given ancestor. Perhaps ancient people sensed the biological significance of that number (how they knew that can be added to the power and mystery of indigenous knowledge). What I do know is considering my mom had six siblings and my dad seven and their parents more, that's a lot of relatives. A lot of relatives who I don't know. I know the names of my grandfathers and grandmothers. I know that I am named after my paternal great-grandmother. With most of my aunts and uncles deceased and my thirty-plus first cousins and dozens of other relatives scattered across the US, Canada, Europe, and Africa, I have lost the connections and stories that tie me to the past. But our shared ancestry lives through me.

It is now understood that there is such a thing as epigenetic as well as genetic information passed down through generations. Genetic information holds our inherited DNA sequence and this does not change. I (presumably) could not have been born with blue eyes because no one in my genetic lineage had them, and nothing about my life will change that. Conversely, epigenetics arise from nongenetic influences. It is being shown that experiences including stress, addiction, anxiety, and fear condition and change heritable traits (positive experiences are also handed down). In labs, mice who learn to associate the smell of cherry blossom with an electric shock become fearful in the presence of the same odor. The children and grandchildren of these same mice are also jumpy and scared when exposed to the smell even though they've never received the electric shock. We can inherit trauma.

Resilience of Seven Generations

Nature is oriented toward wellness.

—DARA WILLIAMS

I cannot count seven generations of my family but I know this: like in all families, there is trauma. Much of it is unspoken. Some I imagine was due to the challenges faced by any lineage of people: natural disasters, loss, tragedy. A lot of it is the result of patriarchy and empire—for much of its history, Ethiopia was a feudal society that encoded the subjugation of women and common people. Trauma was also the result of colonization—both sides of my family lost their traditional interconnection as people dispersed from homelands to cities, adopted European education and norms, and, in the case of my father's family, abandoned indigenous Christianity for Protestant missionary churches. Invasions by Italian fascists brutalized both countries. Eritrea was colonized—my father, born an Italian citizen, was forced to attend Italian schools and venerate Mussolini. Even though the Italians were defeated in Ethiopia and the country was never officially colonized (a great source of pride for us), the Italians occupied it for over five years and staged a reign of terror—violence, torture, rape, and chemical warfare left their mark.

There are addiction and mental health issues on both sides of my family. I feel nervous writing that sentence—except I know that likely every person reading this will be relieved because: you too. Many immigrants are taught to hide personal and community challenges. Our parents and grandparents left homelands so that we could have a better opportunity for education and professional advancement. Gratitude, hard work, and success are the prospects. Within these expectations of excellence, there is no room for the incapacitating results of trauma. But belonging to seven generations gets lost. The net of support and knowing ourselves through a web of relationships cannot be recovered. Tending to that loss as well as the results of collective and individual trauma is part of the work of reclaiming belonging.

For Native Americans and African Americans, the disconnection from the ancestors can often be worse than for those of us who immigrated here. The indigenous people of the US were killed, displaced, and forced into residential schools and reservations. Their land, language, culture, and tradition were forcibly taken from them. African Americans were literally stolen from their land and brutally separated from their cultures and from each other for generations, even after they were settled in this country. Sometimes, knowing where you're from and having some connection to the land from which your ancestors originate can be helpful for a sense of belonging, although not necessarily. Belonging to your people is vital to people from all cultures, and some families maintain strong personal and social connections regardless of their social histories. I know the exact villages my people lived in for centuries, but I feel less belonging to family than some of my African American friends who don't know their ancient origins but attend yearly family reunions with dozens of people filling out their network of connection. There are reasons why we don't feel belonging. Those reasons have both personal and political histories.

And, hey, white people, you have tons of trauma too. Whether you come from the underclass of immigrants from Ireland and Italy, or Jews fleeing the pogroms and the World War II Holocaust, or your family became rich from the enslavement and brutalization of Africans, there is not a human being in this country that is free from the trauma of dislocation, loss, and the general vicissitudes of life (not to mention the heavy trauma of inflicting trauma on others). And there is no going back. There are some exercises at the end of the book inviting you to explore what you know and don't know about where you come from and what that might mean, but very few of us will be able to reconnect the dots so that those seven generations—all the names, all the lives, all the history—are remembered. Where does that leave us moderns?

Indigenous Focusing Oriented Therapy (IFOT) for complex trauma was created by Shirley Turcotte, a Métis elder who combined Focusing techniques with Indigenous Psychotherapy. It is a methodology that utilizes tools and world-views centering land, ancestors, and rituals as part of a system for working with trauma. In this practice, trauma is seen as information and wisdom passed down through the generations. Rather than being in contention with trauma, we develop a relationship with this information so that, as my friend and lead IFOT teacher DaRa Williams says, we can begin to see that under the mess, everything is okay. Taking cues from nature, which is always rebalancing, trauma is not seen as a mistake or a problem, but rather a natural outcome of circumstances.

Experiences of violence and brutality will lead to fear and mistrust within individuals, families, and whole communities. These responses should be expected and—here's the twist—they can be helpful. Fear, anxiety, paranoia, and inhibition are tendencies that traditional Western psychotherapy pathologizes. Indigenous Psychotherapy insists that trauma is actually an outcome of survival and resilience. We can hear the wisdom of our ancestors in our patterns: within them there is medicine. Traumatic patterns are handed down as useful information, as strategies for survival. But like the mice avoiding the cherry blossom scent, we may not need these strategies any longer. With awareness and acceptance, we can understand this information and release what is not needed. Through practice, all of us can begin connecting to the messages imprinted in our very bodies that help guide us to the well-being that is always present. We belong to our ancestors and in fact they are right here within us, helping us belong.

I Don't Belong Here: Releasing Fear

I was struck by a recent interview with the Korean American actress Sandra Oh about being offered the starring role in the series *Killing Eve*. When she received the script from her agent, it never occurred to her that she was up for the lead. As she read the script, she couldn't understand which part she was being considered for. Her agent told her it was for the lead. Oh was shocked at her underestimation of herself. "After being told to see things a certain way for decades, you realize, 'Oh my god! They brainwashed me!' I was brainwashed!" She says she thinks of that moment often, struck by how much she, a supremely successful actress, was still caught in old patterns (of feeling not belonging).

As we begin to know ourselves, we are able to witness these patterns. Feelings of not belonging originate from somewhere. It does not matter whether I know the origins of those feelings. Much of the origin of my feelings of not belonging is unknown or lost. I have deep fears of abandonment (very Enneagram 4). I assume those come from when I was four years old and my father left us for a few years to become a guerrilla fighter in the war for independence in Eritrea. Or maybe my fears come from inherited fears or trauma on one or both sides of family. What I do know is that those experiences will continue to influence and even determine my sense of belonging if they remain unconscious and unresolved. They fuel the semiotic vigilance that keeps me scanning for potential abandonment—an attempt to protect against that possibility. In the past, that looked like interpreting every mood or emotion from a lover as a sign of rejection and preemptively attacking them as a twisted form of defense.

Vigilance is exhausting. And it is rooted in fear. Fear is one of the strongest sensations we can experience. It is biologically programmed to help us respond quickly to perceived threats and therefore to protect us from harm. We evolved fear as a mechanism for good reasons—to keep us safe from danger, from wild animals, and from other threats of early human life. We experience fear every day in small and large ways. This is normal. We need fear to avoid harm: collisions while driving, our children accidentally falling, or danger in new surroundings and situations.

Although some of us live amid real danger and threat, many of us do not experience life-and-death fear regularly. Rather, fear has adapted into habituated responses that affect our ability to be in new situations and take social risks. You may know the statistics that people are more frightened of public speaking than death. Like, dead death. They would rather die than speak in front of an audience. As usual, by *they*, I mean *me*.

I did not have the aspiration to become a teacher. I have always been afraid of speaking in front of people. When I was in grad school, I gave a paper at a conference once. I mean only one time. That was enough. I was extremely nervous before my panel and paced anxiously in an empty room. In an attempt to calm myself down I did yoga poses, including a head stand. No, it did not help. I arrived at the panel and sat down in my seat with my paper in front of me. I looked at no one. I reread the notes I had written in the margins; these would guide my main points. When I finally I looked up, I saw my friend Melissa right in front of me. She was a welcome sight. But my nerves emerged again as the moderator announced my name. I looked again at Melissa. She sensed I was nervous and made a drink gesture with her hands, tipping an imaginary cup to her own mouth and pointed with her eyes at the space on the table in front of me. I looked down and picked up the water someone had set there. My hands were shaking. Visibly. As I followed through on my attempt to deliver this object to my mouth, water splashed from the cup onto my paper blurring my notes. Needless to say, I did not feel I belonged in academia.

Fear can appear in relatively harmless moments (like in front of an audience of nerds). We often experience fear in the form of ongoing worry or unease. Or it can come as a powerful wave of almost overwhelming emotion in response to challenging situations. People have different reasons for developing fear in the world at large or in their own bodies . . . a dark street at night is a very different experience for a woman walking alone or for someone whose sexual orientation or gender identity makes them a target. A traffic stop for a Black person in this country rightfully produces fear that it likely does not for a white person.

And it's not just the threat of physical violence that can make our experience of fear different depending on our experience of the world and the world's experience of us. Our fears are often in the form of anxiety, distress, panic, or trauma. But really, they are still working with the same mechanism—a reaction to some perception of threat, whether or not that threat is real or imagined. Often our fears are not serving us in the way they were meant to: they're not actually protecting us from real harm. They're mostly *imagined* harm. We might mistake a shadow for a falling object once, but if we then brace ourselves against every shadow, we will be moving through the world very jumpy—like those descendant mice smelling cherry blossoms. If you live life perceiving every unknown person as a threat, or every social encounter or every academic challenge or public speaking experience or every potential romantic interaction (or whatever it is you fear) as a threat, as a threatening shadow, life's going to be pretty hard. Knowing ourselves helps us understand our particular patterns. Recognizing that traumas are produced and inherited as protection mechanisms, we can recognize that they can also be released and reclaimed into wellness. But we must see them in the first place. This is why we study ourselves.

Danielle is a mixed-race woman who came to see me as a coaching client. She had spent years developing her visual portfolio while working full-time for a museum. She was fastidious and dedicated to her art, spending hours in her studio in the evenings and on weekends. She arrived at our coaching session wanting to create a plan for her career, to map out her residency applications and an eventual exit from her job. Through the initial sessions, I learned that her intense work ethic left her very little time for friends or fun. And her romantic relationship was suffering. I asked her about this: "Do you have any aspirations for your relationship in coaching or is it only your career you want to look at?"

She thought for a moment, "I guess I don't think about that very much. I'm so consumed with my career."

"Why do you think that is, Danielle?"

She paused with her head tilted down for some time. It was only when she looked up that I saw her eyes were filled with tears. "I don't know who I'd be if I don't make it as an artist."

Danielle and I worked together for a few months. As she opened up to looking at other parts of her life, her coaching focus changed. We shifted away from mapping her art career toward gaining clarity about her aspirations and intentions. She decided cultivating more joy and spontaneity in her life was important to her. Danielle reentered therapy to understand how she had been shaped by the pressure for achievement she felt from her parents (a Black father from Haiti and a white mother from France). Danielle was gripped with a deep fear of disappointing them. Having chosen an unconventional career, she felt guilty about not honoring their sacrifices for her achievements. Fear was feeding her feelings of not belonging, of not being successful enough, of not making her parents proud, of not being worthy of love.

As part of her practice, Danielle journaled daily using the prompt "What is my deepest longing?," which led her to realize she longed desperately for more connection with others. Although she loved painting, Danielle admitted that she did not connect with the people in the art world she'd met so far, so she'd mostly isolated herself. She had been so focused on achieving success, she had buried her longing for nurturing relationships.

Sometimes we will know the original source of our not belonging; often we will not. Our invitation and challenge is to spend time knowing ourselves. Often that means being willing to see what we don't normally see.

What You Don't See:
Spiritual Bypass and Seeing Our Shadows

There are parts of ourselves that are crystal clear. We know those parts; some we may deem positive and some negative, but we *are* aware of them. Then there are other parts that we bury deep within. In some schools of psychology, the shadow is a metaphor for parts of ourselves that we have rejected. Here's one way to look at it: Let's say the persona is the mask we wear to present to the outside world (I'm a meditation teacher; I'm a father; I'm an artist; I'm the boss)—in other words, how we want the world to see us—and the *ego* is our intimate sense of self, or who we are to ourselves (I have this biography; I've had these experiences throughout my life; I'm an angry/sad/happy/confident person), then our *shadows* would be the parts of ourselves that we've disowned, things that we don't see and, in fact, mostly don't *want* to see about ourselves. They include things we reflexively refuse or deny. The shadow contains things about us that are largely, if not entirely, unconscious. But we can work to see and integrate them.

Yes, we also belong to our shadow.

When we're young, the shadow holds the things that our parents, families, communities, and cultures deem unacceptable. Perhaps you received messages that it's not okay to be angry, or openly sexual, or show too much emotion, or be bold or assertive. Or maybe it was really not okay to fail in your family. So, you buried those parts or keep them at bay or pretty tamped down. Or maybe in your family it wasn't okay to be too healthy or too together—a certain amount of dysfunction was the norm (I can certainly identify with that). It's not only so-called negative traits that end up in the shadow—often there's a baseline of what's accepted in a culture, and anything less than or greater than this ends up in the shadow. And sometimes, especially for certain people and groups, it's actually even harder to see and own the positive that's buried in the shadow. In this culture, it can be hard for a woman to exert power—she won't be called "assertive" like a man would, she'll be called overly emotional or "a bitch."

There are different sorting processes for what is acceptable or not depending on a community's norms. We get different messages depending on gender, race, class, size, and personality. In some cultures or communities, it's good to be an individual and stand out and shine; in others, this is seen as negative (egotistical, self-centered, even selfish). In some cultures, it's the norm to be physical and touch people; in others, it's very discouraged. On the receiving end for individuals, especially for kids, much of the sorting process for these messages of what's acceptable and unacceptable can seem quite arbitrary. We can also get different messages from our different caregivers.

Of course, there are reasons why these rules emerged, even if they're mostly lost to us. They create group cohesion and belonging, safety, and trust. But they also get created in the context of oppressive systems. In modern culture, larger forces of power and oppression dictate ways of being for the masses that keep those systems running smoothly. Don't be late, don't be inefficient, keep up with the Jonses by consuming a lot. And marginalized groups intuitively create norms that protect them—many Black parents are extremely strict because misbehaving or talking back for a Black person can lead to harm or even death. Or the rules can change on us if we move in and out of various cultures. Think of what happened to Emmett Till visiting his family down south.

Some of us immigrants bury our languages, ways of moving, and ways of being for the sake of assimilation or acceptance. When I was in high school, I became self-conscious about the spices in our home and began to wear massive amounts of perfume to cover up what I thought was a bad smell on me. Some people rebel and actually choose the shadow as a form of protest, like the sexual openness of the hippies that uncovered the shadow of the fifties' anti-sexuality norms, the anti-assimilationism of the Black Panthers that challenged the shadow of Jim Crow, or drag culture that challenges the shadow of patriarchal gender binaries. But even in communities that are rebelling or have more awareness, we may find that there are also unconscious or unwanted ways of being that get buried. By the time we're adolescents and adults, we've learned what is allowable and not allowable in our given or chosen groups and to some degree we accept and internalize those rules. In the process, we lose our wholeness or our fullness.

Remember, this is largely an unconscious process. By remaining unconscious of these things, we create a split in ourselves. We learn to show some parts and hide others, even from ourselves. There's a fragmentation that's inevitable when we reject things about us—we create what my teachers Thanissara and Kittisaro call "orphans of consciousness." Orphans of consciousness don't completely disappear. They may be buried very deeply, but they're still there. And they do get expressed, somehow. They get expressed in our emotions of shame, fear, or unexpressed rage, but also in our unexpressed joy! On the societal level they get expressed though horror movies, violent video games, and pornography, as well as in more violent and oppressive ways: environmental destruction, economic pillaging, war, rape, and violence. We also project the shadow onto others: immigrants, poor people, Black people, gay men and lesbians, the disabled, trans people, indigenous people.

Which is why it's so important to know yourself and your own shadows. It's not that the shadow is bad—we're not trying to get rid of it. The shadow holds the taboos and agreements that protect a culture. It is vital to belonging: it's not always appropriate to outwardly express our deepest and most difficult concerns. We want to know our shadow, to integrate these things about ourselves, not destroy them. Healthy societies have rich ceremonial processes (rituals, masks, possession) for integrating the shadow. In much of modern life we have lost these processes and instead reject and deny the shadow. How do we see our own personal and collective shadows (and projections)? How do we make the unconscious conscious?

Therapy is one way. Honest friends. Self-exploration. As I detailed above, I've studied many (too many?) self-knowledge systems. And what have I learned? Mostly that I have a long way to go to release the shadow material (that which I try to bury). I have recurring tendencies; I can be a know-it-all; I have an outsized amount of envy (also very Enneagram 4); I have shame around money and privilege. It doesn't always feel good to see this stuff, especially when it sneaks up on me. I also have hidden treasures that I am slow to acknowledge: my ability to attune to others, my affection for almost everyone I meet, my deep well of wisdom.

Lately I've been looking closely at how fear of not belonging ties me to patterns of domination. When I feel unsure about myself or someone else, I can devolve into my patterns of "know-it-allness" (spell check initially corrected "allness" to "illness" . . . apt). When my know-it-all self shows up, I use my intellect to soothe my feelings of isolation, sadness, or disconnection. I will try to out-argue someone or display how much it is I know about something so that I feel better, feel more belonging. Often that can show up as "out-woking" someone, using the guise of justice to distance myself from understanding. In my defense of an oppressed perspective, I seem to be siding with what is right and just. Of course, that's not true belonging, because I'm separating and dominating. Over the years, I have come to see how the need to be right is connected to not belonging. I don't always catch it before it gets expressed or projected, but I'm getting better at knowing and accepting it (and loving it . . . next chapter). Separation begets dynamics of domination. It's easy to see in systems of oppression, where the brutalization of groups of people by this delusion is made structural. It's harder to see that in ourselves on a day-to-day basis.

Your patterns may be different. Mine are too, depending on the situation. When feelings of not belonging are triggered in spaces where I feel intimidated—let's say in a room of powerful or extremely successful people—my patterns emerge as self-judgement. I get quiet and standoffish. My actions are often interpreted as arrogance (further separating me from others and keeping the cycle going). At times, when I'm feeling intimidated, I can deflect to judging others, deeming them privileged or oppressive as a way to assuage my feelings of separation (separation begets domination). I've simply swapped the position of better-than for less-than. None of these tactics truly soothe my experience; they're merely attempts to bypass feelings of not belonging

"Spiritual bypass" is a phrase coined by John Welwood in the 1980s. An American Buddhist teacher and psychotherapist, he developed this concept to describe a phenomenon he noticed among mostly white convert Buddhists (many of whom had studied in Asia). These practitioners often used meditation and Buddhist teachings, especially the transcendent teachings of impermanence, not-self, and emptiness or even the simple concept of letting go to bypass unresolved emotional and psychological issues. He called this "premature transcendence."

Imagine meditating and having anger arise. If we follow the instructions given throughout the book thus far, we would bring an embodied awareness to the anger that allows us to be in relationship with it, not pushing it away. Using kindness and curiosity, we would notice and allow any sensations, thoughts, or emotions. With spiritual bypass, we turn to the absolute as a way to avoid the relative and use meditation or any spiritual teachings to avoid feeling pain or discomfort within or around us. If anger arises, we might ignore or dismiss our feelings by trying to force a sense of calm, oneness, or even an insistence that if we were truly spiritual, we would never get angry (good luck with that). Sometimes it can *seem* like we are letting go, connecting with the light, or are one with all—but all we are doing is avoiding discomfort. As meditation teachers say: "What we resist, persists." Sometimes what we resist is unconscious.

Making the Unconscious Conscious

We call meditation a practice because it's something we attempt and improve at so that we can apply it in our lives. But really, anything is a practice. And anything we practice we get good at, whether what we are practicing is good for us or not: I can practice being swayed by the conditioning of society or I can practice undoing these implicit biases. The latter requires practicing seeing what I don't normally see or making the unconscious conscious. Again, unconscious or implicit biases are learned stereotypes that are unintentional and deeply ingrained. We can have unconscious bias about any number of things: gender, size, class, ethnicity, religion, accents, etc. Race is one of the most studied biases.

Race is not a biological reality, it's a construct. Because this fact is not widely discussed, many people still don't know this. It is undisputed that there is greater genetic variation within "racial" groups than between them, which means race is a social category, not a scientific one. Racial categories are based on skin color, geography, and phenotype and nothing else. Race as we know it today was invented in the eighteenth century to categorize different groups of people in order to justify the slave trade and colonialism. "Race" was created in order to rationalize racism; or as Ta-Nehisi Coates says: "Race is the child of racism, not the father."

There are many people in the medical field who still do not explicitly understand this (I have met a number of them). And there are many more who implicitly buy into racial differences. In 2016 a study of medical students and residents at the University of Virginia found that a substantial number of white medical students and residents held false beliefs about biological differences between Black and white people. These future doctors thought that Black people age more slowly than whites, that their nerve endings are less sensitive than whites', that Black blood (whatever that is) coagulates more quickly than white blood, and that Black skin is thicker than white skin. 2016, not 1916. These residents consciously rejected stereotyping and prejudice, but they unconsciously held unfounded racist pseudoscientific beliefs. Most of us fall sway to unconscious bias.

White doctors who claimed no conscious bias demonstrated unconscious bias toward Black patients. These doctors were less likely to give life-saving drugs to Black patients presenting with heart attack symptoms. Because of these unconscious biases, white people are twice as likely as Black people to receive thrombolytic therapy for heart attacks. These types of disparities are true also for other interventions. There has been a lot of research into the under-prescribing of pain medication based on race and class. I have visited emergency rooms many times over years of cancer treatment. I remember one instance when I waited an excruciatingly long time to receive pain medication. I couldn't understand why the nurse was ignoring my pleas. It turned out my appendix was close to rupturing. Apparently, Black patients are often perceived as "drug seeking." When I learned about this I realized I had probably been on the receiving end of this kind of profiling though at the time I was not aware of it. Black patients receive opioids for severe pain at 60 percent the rate of white patients, and their pain is reassessed less than half as frequently. When they do receive medications, the medications are delivered an average of 32 minutes later than for their white counterparts. In one study, Black children with a clear diagnosis of appendicitis received opioids for severe pain at 20 percent the rate of white children. Imagine the many lives that have been harmed or even cut short by this unconscious behavior.

There has been research exploring the connection between criminal sentencing and "Afrocentric features bias," which refers to the generally negative judgements and beliefs that many people hold regarding individuals who possess Afrocentric features such as dark skin, a wide nose, and full lips. Researchers found that when controlling for numerous factors (seriousness of the primary offense, number of prior offenses, etc.), Black people with the most prominent Afrocentric features received longer sentences than their less Afrocentrically featured counterparts. But this type of bias happens beyond medical settings or courtrooms—it happens at the grocery store, on public transportation, in work spaces. There is proven unconscious rejection of people based on their skin color and appearance—turning away from Black people, not looking them in the eye, disapproving of their behaviors.

These are not conscious decisions. Most of us hold conscious egalitarian values. Why can't we seem to live up to our conscious goals? Trying to tackle bias (and belonging) at only the conscious level alone won't save us. You know why? Here's the REALLY important thing to know about unconscious bias . . . ready? It's *unconscious*. The unconscious, more than the conscious mind, controls our daily decisions and actions, including how we relate to other people, especially those who look different from us. We may have conscious values and aspirations but we are ruled by unconscious beliefs. Knowing ourselves means knowing this, too.

Bias:
Inward and Outward

Ten years ago, I was part of a multiyear training for Buddhist leaders that was about 40 percent people of color and 30 percent LGBTQI. The program had been in existence for years, but this was the first iteration that was so inclusive. On the first day, another Black person noted that all the Black people interacting with white people were "leading with their résumé." I instantly knew what she meant. I had done it a few times already when I met a new white person. I would somehow work into the conversation just how long I'd been practicing (over fifteen years by then), that I'd studied Buddhism academically, and that I'd practiced in Asia. As Black people, we knew the tacit assumption of many white people around inclusive policies: we did not want to be assumed to have been let in *only* because of race. Later that day, a white man said to me offhandedly, "I was on the wait-list, but I guess a Black person dropped out." I don't think he knew he was being offensive. I hope not. People assume that so-called *minorities* (we're the global majority) get where they get not because they deserve it but because standards are being lowered (not raised, mind you) to admit them. This is a common stereotype lodged deep within us by society even when we consciously know better.

"Stereotype threat" is the threat of being viewed through the lens of a negative stereotype, or the fear of doing something that would inadvertently confirm that stereotype. The term was coined by researchers who showed that Black college students performed worse on standardized tests than their white peers when they were reminded before taking the tests that their racial group tends to do poorly on such exams. This can also be true for women and other identities. If you are part of marginalized groups, you don't need to be reminded of negative stereotype, you absorb those messages . . . all the time. Those stereotypes are broadcast by the media, popular culture, politicians, and partners' relatives. In my late twenties, I was on vacation with my (white) boyfriend's family. His parents were academics and we always had interesting conversations about art and literature. I was sitting on the sofa with his mother, a professor of literature. I had been reading *Sula* that week. We started talking about Toni Morrison's many books (none of which she had read) when she suddenly stopped and said, "Don't you think she won the Nobel prize *only* because she is Black?" Toni Morrison. Toni. Morrison. TONI M. F. MORRISON!

Even as much as we remind ourselves that this is conditioning, that this is programmed by the culture, we all have colonized minds (and hearts and bodies) and are conditioned and drawn to the center circle with promises of access and resources. Even when we put that idea right into the name of this term—unconscious bias—we can still act surprised, ashamed, guilty, defensive, even arrogant when our own bias is uncovered. In my experience, the "smarter" you are, the harder this can be for you to understand . . . you smarty-pants think you can think your way out of this. (As usual, I'm talking about myself.)

Two years ago, my older sister Finot was having surgery. Finot can't read or write and has the intellectual level of a young child even though she's very emotionally mature and very joyful. I am her legal guardian but she lives in a wonderful community upstate. I was there for the day before her surgery and stayed with her in the hospital overnight and with her in her home for a few days after. But it was her house leaders where she lives who took her to the pre-op appointments and interfaced with the doctors and hospital leading up to the surgery. Finot's house leader, Nadege, had told me they really liked the surgeon they were working with, Dr. Laborde. She said Dr. Laborde was very sensitive and skilled at explaining everything to Finot in a way that she could understand. The day of the surgery, we were waiting in the pre-op room for Dr. Laborde with other patients and doctors. Except for one Filipino nurse, everyone working in that room was white. Finot's anesthesiologist, a white male doctor came by. The assisting surgeon, also a white man, came and introduced himself. Then Dr. Laborde walked in. Dr. Laborde is a young, dark-skinned Black woman.

I didn't expect that. I knew she was a woman, but I assumed she was white. And I felt so embarrassed by my assumption. So, when I ask the question: Why can't we live up to our conscious values? I am asking myself: Sebene, mindfulness teacher, teacher of unconscious bias, why can't *you* live up to your conscious values?!

I also give you the recent examples of Black female doctors not being believed that they're doctors on Delta flights. Yes, that *is* plural. Not once but twice in the past few years, Black women doctors on Delta flights attempting to attend to sick or distressed passengers have been questioned about whether they are in fact doctors and were prevented from attending to those in need. Look it up. The details of these encounters are ridiculous. In one, Dr. Fatima Cody Stanford even showed the flight attendants her medical license, but she was still disbelieved. Dr. Stanford carries her medical license everywhere for exactly this reason. My friend Lore is a mental health counselor in a small Massachusetts town. She had a white male client who was quite delusional and believed himself to be a medical doctor. He went around everywhere proclaiming this. And guess what—he was always believed (no ID needed).

The mind gets lost in stereotypes because that is often the only information available to it. Consider for a moment the thousands of hours of television and media you've watched. For those of us of a certain age, the majority of Black roles were servants or criminals. We had to make the conscious effort to seek out information to challenge these stereotypes. That is changing. The Black comedian W. Kamau Bell tells the story of his young daughter who obsessively watched the animated show *Doc McStuffins* about a young Black girl who plays doctor to her stuffed animals and whose own mother is a doctor. When Bell's daughter went for a checkup, she had a hard time believing the white man who walked in could be a doctor. But unconscious biases still exist in the most well-intentioned people and have severe consequences when we are not consciously tending to their dismantling. Doctors, judges, or people simply walking their dogs in the park can cause harm and even death when these biases are left unchecked.

It takes the work of each of us to look at our minds and hearts to begin to uncover unconscious biases and connect from a place of conscious awareness. This means being willing to look at the parts of ourselves that we don't usually see. And accepting that we might not like what we find. When we start seeing our biases and conditioning toward ourselves and others, it can sometimes overwhelm us with bad feelings. Meditation practice teaches us to stay with any discomfort. As we learn to be with what's inside, it makes riding the bumpy roads of life a whole lot smoother.

Smoothing the Axle Hole

Those who cannot change their minds cannot change anything.
——GEORGE BERNARD SHAW

I love the metaphors in Pali, the language of early Buddhist teachings. There's an essential word, *dukkha*, often translated as "suffering." *Dukkha* refers to all the ways life is imperfect, unsatisfactory, and painful. This encompasses the pain that is inevitable: the loss, illness, and difficulties that are an unavoidable part of being alive. It also describes the suffering we cause (and the freedom we deny) ourselves because we are in contention with pain: this is perhaps the most important teaching for understanding the freedom of belonging. In Pali, *dukkha* is itself a metaphor. *Kha* is the axle hole of a wheel and the prefix *du-* means bad (*su-* is good). So *dukkha* is a bad or crooked axle hole (*sukkah* being a good axle hole—smooth, round, spacious). *Dukkha* comes to mean suffering or stress or lack of ease. *Sukkah* is often translated as "happiness." We can think of *dukkha* or suffering as being a bad or bumpy ride.

We can also extend this metaphor. If we are the wheel, smoothing out our own axle hole is our responsibility. The road may be bumpy: other people, the weather, the political mess happening. The road may be smooth—a beautiful day, vacation, no money worries—but if we have a crooked axle hole, the ride will be bumpy. Even if there are bumps in the road (or even craters—which there will be), our ride will be smoother if we work on our own axle hole.

A silent retreat is a perfect example to explore the potential of this metaphor. Imagine a beautiful location, comfortable accommodations, no obligations, no communications, delicious meals, a spacious schedule, and time to just be. Now imagine being with your own mind for hours on end, day after day, even week after week. Smooth road, potential bumpy ride. At least that has been my experience. I have had both challenging and wonderful rides on retreat. The contrast was entirely about my own wheel.

On one long silent meditation retreat, I experienced intense agitation and anxiety. Those of you who have done retreats know that it is possible for the mind to become quite still and spacious—or not. My lack of ease on this particular retreat was spilling over into my experience outside of formal practice—becoming annoyed by other people, being disgruntled about the food options, and obsessing over situations from the past (completely gone) or the future (totally imagined). I was having a bumpy ride. I could sit there all day every day with my blabbering, deluded mind going on and on. But the only real possibility for creative response and for transformation was to invite kindness, get curious, cultivate ease, and smooth my own ride. So that's what I practiced.

Rather than spin in my frustration, I used embodied awareness to reconnect to my felt sense. I spent many hours simply being with the breath in the belly. I was having allergy-induced coughing and sneezing sitting in the hall, so I lay down in my room to make meditation more easeful. My persistent thinking did not magically disappear, but I tried not to add more agitation by becoming frustrated with my thinking mind. I simply acknowledged the thoughts and gently brought my awareness back to the breath. I connected with the least constricted part of the breath, relating to what was most easeful in any moment. I periodically connected with the feeling of my back against the floor, sensing that contact with the ground. Later, after I had cultivated some groundedness and calm indoors, I did this practice outside, laying down on one of the walking paths amid the wildflowers, allowing the Earth to hold me.

Avoiding persistent feelings, ignoring our patterns, and not knowing ourselves is like driving around on a broken wheel and blaming the road. If we avoid fixing our wheel, we are going to experience a lot of bumpy rides. Or to mix metaphors: If we are in a shared ocean—as we've experienced in the coronavirus pandemic—we must tend to our own boats in order to ride out any rough waves (plugging holes, bailing water). We can't control the waves, but we can try to not capsize.

Of course, if we work on our wheel, smoothing it out and making sure we can have the smoothest ride possible, we will still encounter bumps out there on the roads of life. We may need to slow down and drive carefully. Even then, we need to continually tend to our wheels because of the wear and tear of life (the roads). Yes, some of us have clear and easy roads and still have bumpy rides because we are in contention with our experience. But different people have different roads. Whole communities have shitty roads. We may want to help others with road repair, but our efficacy will be directly proportionate to our self-knowledge. We must know ourselves (and our own roads). We must take time to understand our patterns, and rather than avoid them, we must meet them, tend to them, and smooth them so that we can bring the most easeful presence to whatever is happening, wherever and whoever we are. Belonging is the smooth ride that is possible in any moment.

Who Are You Really?

Like many teens, my youngest nephew is often glued to his gadgets, playing games. A few years ago, he went through a phase where he insisted you sit behind him and watch his avatar accumulate points. I did my auntie-duty because I want him to feel seen by me. We all have that desire to be seen . . . except when we don't.

Every retreat I ask myself the same question: "How can I be so completely fascinated by myself and so utterly sick of myself almost in the exact same moment?" I spend most of my time in meditation thinking about me. Also, I complain about me to me. I like to think of this as the "narcissistic paradox of practice." All of us have that chasm between the desire to be seen (when we feel good about ourselves) and the desire to disappear (when we don't). Meditation practice is about learning to see our whole selves compassionately. To do this, we need to study the self. When things are "going good" (peaceful, positive), we might enjoy "studying the self." When things are going to shit (turbulent, troubled), not so much. Often, we come to practice wanting to get rid of parts of ourselves. If we want only the "good stuff" or reject things we don't like, we can't know ourselves in full.

As Dōgen said, this knowing of the self leads to a forgetting of the self. What does it mean to "forget the self" in a selfie society, in an economic climate where everyone is a brand (hello, my name in big letters on the cover of this book), in a world that erases or distorts your cultures? Can you see your self? Just as you are, right now? Who are you, really? It's a package deal, studying and forgetting the self. We know ourselves through our ancestors, our experiences, and through our connection to everything around us. The less wrapped up we are in our patterns—reactively avoiding pain or acting out unconscious conditioning—the more available we are for whatever life presents. As we forget the self, we remember that we are part of a whole. We can't have a connection to everything if we're trying to get rid of the self that is the very vehicle to experience connection. That's why loving ourselves is so important.

Love Yourself

Every chapter in this book could have been titled "Love Yourself"—all the pages filled with one sentence, repeated over and over: Love yourself. Love yourself. Love yourself. This imperative is the motto of belonging. Our sense of freedom and joy depends on it. When we truly love ourselves, we don't need to be someone or something else. When we love ourselves, our sense of separation softens, the need to dominate dissolves. Comparison and competition clear away in the presence of self-love. Hierarchy and oppression crumble. We belong.

As we've explored, children learn how to be and not to be in order to fit in. As kids, we absorb society's dictates and prescriptions. We don't want to experience rejection so we limit being too different. We long for those physical features, personal characteristics, or material objects we *think* will bring us belonging. Especially us immigrants, misfits, and weirdos, we learn the ways of dressing and speaking, and the codes of behavior that will gain us acceptance. Some of us see through the dominant culture's hierarchies and rebel against them in an attempt to belong. We find countercultural groups and realities, which have us judging ourselves through new rules of belonging. Part of being human is our need to belong to groups, and modernity requires grappling with the complexity of multiple identities and affiliations—which can lead to the semiotic vigilance of not belonging. We judge and police everything about ourselves. To directly challenge our tendency for near-constant self-abnegation, we must choose a fierce, uncompromising self-love rooted in the certainty of belonging.

Love yourself. This is not about simply tolerating what we don't like about ourselves, bearing our faults and challenges as if they are our deserved punishment. Loving yourself asks you to affirm and care for every part of your body, to adore all aspects of your personality, and to appreciate your experiences and current life circumstances. Cherish the things you deride: your temper, your cellulite, your depression, your physical limitations, your jealousy. You are not only *not* in contention with life, you are grateful for it all. Be grateful to everything, including past difficulties that got you to this moment: your family dysfunction, *that* relationship, your career fails. Nothing is a mistake or a problem. Do not reject any part of you. It's not that you long to perpetuate every dubious characteristic. You're not loving *envy*; you love yourself even when you *feel* envy, recognizing that it served you in some way. I can love myself even when I don't like what it is I think, feel, or do—I can love myself in every moment (not just those I approve).

Adore yourself. Imagine starting each new day filled with this devotion for your being, greeting each day with the simple invitation to allow love. Allow love to flow to all the parts of your life. And as you allow love for yourself, love for everything else will follow, in time. Right now: Love yourself. Love yourself. Love yourself.

Gratitude helps.

Grateful for It *All*

Gratitude is a practice. I practice with my friend Lynn. Every morning, we text each other three things for which we are grateful: people, places, things, experiences. Each day, I discover the many parts of my life and of the world that I appreciate: the colors of sunset I see from my kitchen window, licks from my dog Suki, chatting with my neighbors in the elevator. It can be challenging to think of new things to text to Lynn and not write "matcha" every day (I wrote "matcha" today). It's even harder to appreciate myself as part of the process. Lynn and I almost always name things external to ourselves. While writing this chapter, I began to text only about aspects of myself for which I'm thankful, including "problem" parts. I didn't tell her what I was doing, I simply offered thanks, even for what I usually reject. It felt uncomfortable at first and then I hit my stride.

My hot flashes. My love of art. My middle-aged body.

My writing practice. My procrastination. My paranoia.

My awkwardness. My envy. My eye for beauty.

My cancer. My scars. My strong teeth.

My cellulite. My swollen arm. My kindness.

My self-care. My anxiety. My bravery.

My confused musings. My discipline. My distraction.

It's hard to love ourselves in moments when we can't stand how we are. I don't enjoy being awkward. I don't like seeing my domineering tendencies (which I usually do only after the fact). I don't love when my pent-up anger seeps out over the phone at an unsuspecting stranger working their exhausting customer service shift. But I've learned to pause and invite a different response to these parts: when I notice a reaction or tendency that I want to push away or banish, I try and soften around it simply by giving it some attention and space. Not rejecting these things is the first step into a deep process of self-love. Loving ourselves is about what my teacher and friend Tara Brach calls "radical acceptance." Simple acceptance can imply acquiescence or bargaining: *I will accept this flaw, defect, or bad habit in order for it to go away.* Radical acceptance invites a deep appreciation for every damn thing about ourselves. Tara offers "this too" as a mantra: *This awkwardness. This domination dynamic. This anger. This too. Love myself.*

Loving ourselves is as much an undoing as a doing. The love is available. Always. Inside and outside. And yet because we are conditioned into the delusion of separation, love is not our default operating mode. In separation, we reject parts of ourselves, other people, and experiences. We don't allow love because of all the barriers created to block it. Those barriers are our attempt to block pain, but they block the love, too. We must allow ourselves to feel it all.

Love may feel like too strong of a word for some of you (see, we even reject *love*). **Get over it.** Belonging will not happen through rejection or hatred. Because, well, that's ridiculous. Belonging inherently *is* love. To belong means to love. Love is what is needed to soothe any sense of not belonging. How can we fully belong if we reject any part of ourselves? To belong means opening to it all.

Love It All

Loving ourselves is the simplest instruction so far. It does not involve the multiple steps of a meditation practice in grounding. Loving does not require the unearthing of experiences in knowing. To love ourselves, we simply *allow love*. Simple, but not easy. There's an apocryphal story about the first time His Holiness the Dalai Lama taught in the US. Someone asked him a question about self-hatred. The story goes that it took ten minutes to even translate the question because the Dalai Lama could not understand the concept of not loving oneself. It seems that within his experience of Tibetan life, this rejection of self did not exist. It may be true of some people and of some traditional cultures—that within the matrix of close-knit families or communities, self-acceptance is easier. Maybe. I don't really know if ancient people had more self-love or what it feels like to grow up in a context where love of self is unquestioned. What I do know is that in the culturally complex context and diasporic diversity of life today (plus the onslaught of media and advertising that insists we need to be different in order to be loved) loving yourself is not so easy.

I constantly evaluate myself physically. Often, that's the easiest judgement to see—especially as a woman. Some parts of me I've learned to reject based on the hierarchies of society, like my middle-aged belly. This is obvious internalized oppression: fat phobia has me policing my body for any signs of weight gain, and that is ridiculous and insidious. Not everyone is swayed by these dominant values. You might be thinking, *Oh, I don't subscribe to fashion ideals and I reject the oppressive messages of our society.* Okay, great and… check in to make sure you're not missing the unconscious and persistent barriers to self-love that mask themselves as "love in opposition." Maybe explore the way self-love can become dependent on comparison and competition *against* the mainstream. As in, we love ourselves because we are more woke or because we reject who we used to be. True self-love will allow us to feel belonging wherever we go, with whomever we are, however we got to this moment. Loving yourself means also loving where you came from. Any time I reject parts of myself, an opportunity to allow love presents itself. This means loving the parts I don't like.

I've been trying to get rid of aspects of my personality ever since I've known me. I reject things that don't measure up to my ideals— the ways I think I *should* be. I am my fiercest critic. At times, I feel that I'm doing it all wrong: *I'm rarely as present as I think I should be, I was not as kind as I should have been, I'm being lazy because I should be productive.* I have some idealized vision of myself that is always more mindful and compassionate and wiser than the current me: *that* me isn't unkind or judgemental, she doesn't get snippy, she does not build walls between herself and others. I analyze and doubt my past experiences and my future deliberations (and miss the present). This constant self-monitoring is wrapped in the belief that I'm not doing enough nor being enough (in reality, I'm often doing too much and I am *always* enough). The self-evaluation is relentless—there's barely room for self-love.

So, how *do* we open up to loving ourselves at all times? We don't. That would be utterly exhausting. And probably impossible— we're not trained for that. It would be like me trying to run a marathon tomorrow. But I can open to loving myself bit by bit, over and over—training for the marathon in stages (and then continuing the training once it's over lest I get out of shape again). This involves letting in love whenever possible—against the tide of unabating messages of being unlovable. It's impossible to truly love ourselves if we never measure up to the impossible standards of beauty, wealth, and accomplishment. If we believe there is a lack, that something is wrong with us, loving ourselves will be impeded. We start loving ourselves by first filtering out demands of fashion and mass media, the pressure for new objects pushed on us by advertising, and the punishing pace of the on-all-the-time work culture.

Anything I do not love about myself plays into the delusion of separation. Why would I not adore every single thing that got me to this moment typing this sentence, breathing this breath, including the ignorance and mistakes of my past? Not belonging is perpetu-ated when I cannot love this very moment and all the moments to come (my aching back *and* my healthy body). I learn to love rather than reject myself. And, most importantly, I love myself even when rejecting myself. This type of all-encompassing loving takes prac-tice and patience. We are so used to judging ourselves and wanting to excommunicate anything we don't like even though it keeps us in not belonging. Allow love, over and over.

Allow Love

About fifteen years ago, I was on a silent meditation retreat. I had been practicing for over a decade but I had not yet started leading meditation or teaching. Having always been nervous in front of groups, I balked when asked to be the practice leader at a morning sitting period. This did not involve very much: simply sit silently at the front of the room of seventy or so people and ring the bell at the end of forty-five minutes. It seemed like a big stretch for me. Since adolescence, many people perceived me as confident, even arrogant. This always puzzled me. Did they not realize I was a teeming mess of insecurity and self-doubt? People scared me, especially white people. But also, Black people. Even Ethiopian people. Okay—everybody. There was only one other Black person on the retreat and no other visible people of color besides the retreat manager, my friend La who had asked me to lead. When I mentioned my nervousness to them, they said, "Sweetie, all you have to do is ring the bell." Oh. Right.

So, I agreed to do it. When the time came, I felt a wave of nervous energy as I made my way up to the stage and onto the cushion recently occupied by a teacher I greatly admire. As I settled into my seat, I could sense the energy in my chest. It was pulsing and tight. I attempted to breathe into it but, as I looked out at the group, I heard a voice in my head. *They don't think you deserve to be up here.* I know this voice. It's loud and bossy. Then it morphs. It's cool and calm. It vigilantly scans for evidence then tells me stories. It consistently insists that I do not belong. Do you know this voice? Maybe it's many voices? A chorus? A shitty chorus. Out of tune and singing really mean covers of cheesy pop songs. *"I'll Be Mocking You." "I Hate You Babe."*

Sitting at the front of a large room of mostly white people meditating, I felt this disruptive message over and over: *They don't think
you deserve to be up here.* All the previous peer leaders had been white,
mostly older. Stereotype threat kicked in: *People assume I was asked to
lead only because I am Black, that I don't know anything about Buddhism,
that I am not a good meditator.* I wanted to tell them just how long I had
studied and practiced. To prove that I was worthy of being here. At
one point my mind was such a jumble of thoughts and projections that
I began to count my breaths to try and recenter myself. At the end of
the session, I rang the bell. As I bowed to those in front of me, I could
sense the relief to not be at the front of the room any longer.

At the end of the retreat, silence was broken in small groups
where people shared about their retreat experience. I was the first
to share with my four white partners. I talked about my fear of
peer-leading and my concern that people would be judging me up
there as a young Black woman and wonder why I was chosen. I
talked about the insecurity about my capacities and achievements as
a meditator and as a person. I had barely finished speaking when a
white woman—a lawyer close to my age—spoke up. "That's funny
you say that because when I first saw you go up there, I thought to
myself: *Does she know she's not supposed to be up there?* I thought you
didn't know that space was only for teachers." Did she really think
I had just wandered up there? Sheesh, it was worse than I thought.
People didn't think I was merely unqualified, they thought I was
stupid, too. It was so absurd I had to laugh. She laughed too, although
I'm sure not for the same reasons.

A few years later I returned to the same retreat community and
once again served as a practice leader. Remembering the previous
incident, I could feel the sense of sadness and grief in my belly. It

sat like a hot pot of simmering hurt. It bubbled up into my chest. I felt the sensations and breathed deeply into the intensity. I simply allowed the sensations, meeting them with some compassion: *this too*. After a few minutes, I sensed it dissipate. I continued to feel my chest rising and falling with each breath until the heat and tension were gone. Only then did I remember the shirt I was wearing. A black t-shirt given to me by my friend Jacky, it said in white letters across my chest: *Allow Love*. I giggled to myself. Of course. All these people are also filled with hurts and pain and longing as well as love. I invited myself to allow all of it. It softened me and I felt ease and calm enter my system.

I can't say why the woman from that first retreat assumed I did not belong at the front of the room, but that room, those types of rooms, every room, *is* filled with love because every human has love inside whether that love is covered over or shining brightly. Which means those rooms are also filled with every person's conditioning. The conditioning of dominant society, our cultures, our families, and our individual patterning. I continue to meet both wherever I go. Conditioning. And love. I choose to make love the conditioning.

Chikko and the Man: Loving the Committee

Loving yourself begins to counter what is called the "inner critic." That makes it sound like we each have *one*—I wish. I myself have a committee. Inner critics are the internal voices that judge and critique us. The commentary can be so constant you don't even notice the persistent punctuation of insults. I have learned over the years not to encourage my inner critics, not to believe them, and (here's the trick) not to hate them. In fact, I have come to love them. You can too.

Within the philosophy of Indigenous Focusing (IFOT), inner critics are considered the wise voices of our ancestors. Our ancestors endured domination or oppression by creating ways of being that protected them and ensured survival. *Keep my head down, cause few problems, don't trust outsiders, be secretive.* These were wise directives— guarding oneself could potentially decrease the chances of being a target of oppression. Remember, in the IFOT perspective, all trauma and tendencies that are handed down through the generations are knowledge. One example is those of us whose sexuality is shut down or repressed. This may be influenced by the larger mores of society. There could also be an element of ancestral knowing—because sexual violence existed as an inevitability throughout history, learning to subdue that expression might mitigate that violence. We can decide to let go of a particular behavior that no longer serves our well-being, but first we must honor the wisdom in what was gifted us.

Even in this lifetime, inner critics develop initially as survival strategies, monitoring and prescribing ways of behaving that allow us to stay safe, get love, and find well-being. I conformed to my family dynamics by not speaking up or expressing needs; in fact, I would simply shut down. To keep the domestic balance, my inner critics kept my anger and upset in check (and helped keep the peace at home). This strategy is no longer useful—now it just leads to me bottling up emotions (and running resentful scripts in my head). As an adult, I have had to learn (and am still learning) how to skillfully express what was for so long the inexpressible. By contrast, my husband, Frederic, grew up in a very political leftist home where arguing was expected. He developed an inner critic that requires he always have the right answer and that can keep him locked in endless (loud) debate. Heated exchanges exhaust me. To this day, I have to bring awareness to the part of me that checks out when conversations start to become contentious. Breathing deeply helps.

Inner critics don't only develop from our home environments, they also demand we conform to society's precepts. For years, I've been followed around stores by security (yes, it still happens). Once, I was chased out of a health food store by an owner accusing me of shoplifting (I dumped my bag out on the sidewalk in a fit of rage in response). Growing up, my inner critics prescribed and monitored a code of behavior in mostly white public spaces that has me purchase something in a café even if I'm waiting for a friend (see #StarbucksWhileBlack).

I was once on a nine-day self-guided retreat. Nine days of listening to what Maria Popova calls the "Stockholm syndrome of the superego." On this retreat, I observed (once again) just how mean my inner critics can be and how much they limit me. There's one critic that goes on and on about what a bad meditator I am, how I have terrible concentration, and how all my insights are shallow. This script inevitably leads me to greater striving. The striving leads to frustration (because, go figure, ease and freedom don't come from grasping desperately at a goal). In my frustration, the critic starts all over again about me being a failed meditator. That voice is such a jerk. But I'm the one who keeps listening to it.

It can be really difficult to determine what's our own intention, and what's the culture's influence. Am I doing something because I have a wholesome aspiration to practice meditation or because I crave the validation of attainment taught to me by our competitive culture? Learning to distinguish who is speaking when takes some sorting. On that retreat, I resolved to determine which voices were which by giving my inner critics names. I wanted designations that exemplified the nagging persistence of these voices but also acknowledged that I was internalizing the messages I was receiving from society. So, I'd like to introduce you to my inner critics: Chikko and The Man (if you don't know seventies sitcoms, google *Chico and the Man*).

Chikko is an Amharic word that can be translated as a nagging or persistent person (the consonants are glottalized or explosive, which makes it sound that much better). When I was little, my mom would lovingly use it when I asked a question too many times or repeated something over and over—"*anchi chikko*" (you nag). Chikko sounds like me, which means she can be logical and erudite, funny and charming. She presents good arguments and has little tricks for getting me to listen to her. Often, she seems to be protecting me from potential danger or disappointment. She "just wants me to have a fruitful retreat." The Man? Well, he's THE Man (duh). He's often writing the scripts that Chikko reads because it's his culture I/we swim in. His scripts are often garbage.

The great Martiniquais psychiatrist-philosopher Frantz Fanon said, "To speak a language is to take on a world, a culture." We are shaped by the culture around us and it shows up in, well, how we show up (*parce que, le colonialisme*). Sometimes it is incredibly difficult for me to untangle my aspirations and motivations from our larger culture of separation and domination. This can manifest in my meditation practice as striving or trying to get somewhere. In the name of spiritual development, I beat myself up for my lack of achievements.

But, remember, there is also wisdom in these critics. I did not develop much discipline growing up. As a latchkey kid, it was up to me to do my homework or not (all through elementary school it was mostly not), to practice violin (definitely not), to cultivate hobbies (nope), even to choose colleges (I only applied to one school. Good thing I got in!). But Chikko and (especially) The Man helped me do enough to keep up at school and in the world in order to be successful. I can't play a single note on the violin but I learned to excel in middle school and beyond because my inner critics were demanding that I keep up with peers and in society. Excelling at things is not important in and of itself, but it opened my possibilities by connecting me to ideas and opportunities I might otherwise have never discovered. It's at that one college where I first read Black feminist theory and began my studies of Buddhism. Can I honor those critics while also not buying into their bullshit?

This is just the beginning. The process of untangling ourselves from our inner critics is, well, a process. Noticing them is the first step. Naming them can help. Understanding—not hating—them is good. Maybe I can even love them. I definitely need to get used to them. Mine have been around for a long time. As much as I try to hit mute, interrupt the broadcast, cancel the show . . . they're still on the air. Sometimes I change the channel and find a new script.

Loving All of Ourselves:
Black Is Beautiful

We are constantly receiving messages from society about what is lovable and what is not. We are told which parts of ourselves are worthy of adoration, how we should behave to be loved, and who and what is attractive. If we don't fit the norms of society, often what is deemed lovable is outside ourselves. Sometimes, society deems us the least lovable of all. But to love oneself is to love everything. There's no loving one part and dismissing the rest. There's no "if only" with love.

Twenty years ago, I traveled to Thailand to visit my best girlfriend, Naomi, who was working as a curator in Bangkok. After a few days touring the capital, we took a trip to Kanchanaburi. The travel there was long, hot, and humid. We dressed in light, loose t-shirts and skirts. On our way, we passed a group of construction workers repairing a bridge. All of them wore denim jeans, heavy long-sleeve shirts, and dark balaclavas covering their entire heads. I looked at Naomi and made a "WTF?" gesture. She said flatly, "They don't want to get any sun on their skin." That was when it really hit me—hatred of dark skin is a global phenomenon.

In most brown families with varying shades of skin tone, beauty is ranked (um, in case there's any confusion: lighter skin wins). Growing up in DC, my mother, my siblings, aunts, uncles, cousins, and most Ethiopian family friends were all lighter skinned than me. On summer trips to the Maryland seashore, my skin inevitably darkened and I would hear opposing opinions about this. Some of my adult family members and their friends would tell me to stay out of the sun. "You're dark enough," they would say (what they wanted to say was "You're too dark already"). My mom and others (mostly my dad's colleagues or grad students from Howard University) would proclaim "Black is beautiful!" One time, we returned from the beach and my mother took me aside. She showed me photos of people from the Gambella region of southern Ethiopia whose skin is darker than mine and whose features have wider noses and thicker lips. With conviction, she talked about these people's beauty. Although I rejected other aspects of my body or features, thanks to the Black Power movement and my mom, I never had a desire to be lighter skinned, even when I was a spectacle.

Many Asian people (especially women) cover themselves during the day, wearing large hats and gloves and carrying umbrellas so that their skin will not darken. Traveling in Southeast Asia for months, I was constantly in the sun. I got very, very dark and very used to being stared at. This was 2000. There were not many other Black tourists there. In Siem Reap near Angkor Wat, Naomi and I watched a woman nearly crash her bicycle because she was so distracted by me and my blackness.

Naomi went back to work after two weeks and I traveled on my own through Thailand. While I was on a ferry between Surat Thani and Ko Samui, a dark-skinned man in his thirties was staring at me intently. He approached smiling and speaking quickly in Thai. I could not understand what he was saying but he was very happy about it. He pointed to his arm and then my arm. He touched his face and then my face. And then he said in English over and over again smiling deeply, "Same same, same same."

Many people of color know the admonishment to stay out of the sun. It is something we can hear from our own families and communities whether we are African American, Indian, Brazilian, or Chinese. Colorism (a nicer way to say hatred for dark skin) reveals within us a lack of love for ourselves. On that trip, in addition to Thailand, I visited Cambodia, Indonesia, and East Timor. I felt my Black skin was an object of fascination primarily because I did not wear it with shame (Thank you, Mommy!). I sunbathed while others cowered. I gloried in the sun (isn't that what the sun wants us to do?).

I have traveled all over the world. And what is ubiquitous in every local market? Skin lightening cream (also: knockoff designer handbags). The global skin-lightening industry is worth billions of dollars and is expected to grow to almost $10 billion in the next ten years, primarily fueled by the Asian market. People (mostly women) slather their skin with dangerous chemicals in the hopes of reaching (white) beauty ideals of fair skin. It's hard to love yourself when so many people hate the very thing that covers your entire body, your largest organ. This has many people reaching for poisonous creams to erase what is unloved all over them. It has them reaching for whiteness.

As I mentioned earlier, the term "reaching for whiteness" is from Pastor Michael McBride. This term makes me feel seen, but not in a good way. Even if my mom helped me accept my darker skin, when I was younger, I wished for a nose like hers, which was thinner. My mom was quite beautiful, but why would I want her nose? Why would I want a nose different than the one I have? A thinner nose looks more like the standard image many have of Ethiopians. A thinner nose also conforms to white ideals of beauty. A thinner nose is one of the many ways I was (and, sigh, sometimes still am) reaching for whiteness. I was taught to reach for whiteness by reaching for wealth and status and standard ideas of beauty. All of us are kept reaching for something that is not us: lighter skin, more money, fame, a different accent, thinness. Whiteness can be used as a metaphor for dominant culture, for the individualism of separation and domination. We are taught to not love our hair texture, our learning style, our fat, our clothes. Whiteness is everyone trying to make it to the center circle by rejecting what connects them to the margins.

The Supremacy of Whiteness

I found god in myself and I loved her, I loved her fiercely.
—NTOZAKE SHANGE

When I was in elementary school, our next-door neighbor Mrs. Higgins worked for President Jimmy Carter. It was just after the energy crisis, when TV images of gas lines snaking along roads and highways dominated the news. The White House planned a Youth Energy Conservation Day and Mrs. Higgins invited all the neighborhood kids to attend. The special event would be hosted by First Lady Rosalynn and their daughter, Amy, with appearances by Captain America and Spider-Man (and Stan Lee). I knew I would wear my favorite dashiki.

I loved my dashiki, proudly displaying the brown and blue, red and ochre pattern in my third-grade class picture. Even though it wasn't Ethiopian, I connected it to Africa and the "Black is beautiful" chants I heard from my father's graduate students. I associated mine with those worn by the African artists and intellectuals who frequented our living room on long weekend nights, when they smoked cigarettes, drank whiskey, and argued politics into the early morning. I loved to wear my dashiki over a blue turtleneck and with brown cords. With freshly braided hair, it was the perfect outfit.

We were told to gather after school the day of the White House event. Mrs. Chapman would be driving us. The Chapman house was on the other side of the Higgins house. Mr. Chapman parked his Mercedes in the garage while the rest of us parked our Fords and Chevys on the street. The Chapman family was the only one on our block for whom I did not babysit.

Mary Chapman was one of the youngest kids on the block. She rarely played with the rest of us but one year, she developed a strong crush on my handsome brother. She lingered in our yard as Asgede taught me to ride his unicycle, watching him carefully as he instructed me to use the dogwood as a balancing pole. One day Mary admitted to me that she liked Asgede, "even though he is a nigger." Her brother, Tim, was two years younger than me. A nonathletic, pensive child, he could often be found waiting at our front door, with Princess Leia, Darth Vader, and Han Solo clutched in his small hands. Sometimes Tim would dare to knock and ask if I could come out to play. Some days, we would go to his backyard and clean the rabbit cage, letting the bunnies roam in the backyard, chasing them around the flower beds when it was time to return them to their wood and wire home.

The day of the event, my sister and I met everyone at the Chapman car. We each had neat, lovely plaits and my sister wore a white turtleneck and light blue bell-bottom jeans. The boys and Mary gathered together and Mrs. Chapman surveyed us all. She smiled at each person until she got to me. Eyeing my shirt, she made a subtle frown. "Liam, Kevin, Josh, Noah, Tim, Finot, you all look very nice today." Subtle she was not.

I would like to say that I wore my dashiki every day for the rest of that year. I did not. I probably tucked it away in the back of a drawer somewhere, where it was easily pushed into a corner in a crumpled ball. I undoubtedly went back to playing dodgeball out back, always aware of the borders defining our untended yard from the manicured gardens around us. Maybe I lay in the grass, dreaming of a different life, one where my parents read me fairy tales and sang me lullabies and where bunnies roamed our perfectly tended lawn.

As a child, I did not consciously evaluate privilege or oppression in the dynamics around me, I simply reached for whatever gained me acceptance. Shy and withdrawn around white people, my mom struggled to navigate the world around us. So, I attached myself to those who did seem able to function well in it (i.e., wypipo). After the dashiki rejection, I wanted Polo shirts and OP shorts. Not trusting my mother's choices, I asked to go shopping at malls where I could find clothes similar to my friends' at school. Regardless of what was going on inside them (probably also a sense of separation and not belonging), the white people around me looked like models for success and achievement. I longed to master that world. I looked for acceptance outside: in places, practices, traditions, and in assimilation, collusion, adaptation. We learn not to love the things others spurn. I reached for what seemed to get love: good grades, good hair, good behavior, easier to pronounce names, predefined beauty, labels . . . being white.

I began to succumb to white supremacy.

My friend Dan doesn't think I should use the phrase "white supremacy" in this book. Oops, oh well. Dan is white (wait, did I need to mention that?). His reasoning comes from his care for me, and his desire for this book to be successful. He thinks I should simply stick to "whiteness" to describe the ways in which safety, success, beauty, intelligence, and status in general are associated with white people. Dan believes most (white) people are turned off by the phrase "white supremacy" (let's prove him wrong, white readers!). Although some white people are already very comfortable with this term and some are getting there, there's still a discomfort for many. For white readers (or anyone else) turned off by the phrase, here's your chance to understand why it's important to our collective sense of belonging.

Whiteness is a racial category that exempts itself from race. People of color are racialized. Whiteness is simply the norm. Whiteness is defined through exclusion. Exactly who is excluded has changed over time. Especially in the US, whiteness shifted to accommodate various social priorities. Often to control labor or resources, different ethnicities and cultural groups in America have been or not been "scientifically" categorized as white (or as multiple inferior and superior white races: Anglo Saxons above Celts above Northern Italians above Southern Italians, and so on). Eventually, all Europeans entered into the primarily flat category of "white." White stands in opposition to the racialized categories of Black, Asian and Pacific Islander, Native American/Indigenous, and Latino, which are to this day promoted by the dominant culture as inferior, either through lack of representation and/or through negative tropes. Even when we've made all the sacrifices, done all the things, reached as far as we can possibly stretch our brown arms, people of color (especially Black people) will still be denied access to whiteness. It's always held out of reach because it is in fact unreachable, inaccessible . . . supreme. Whiteness is so preferred, people will bleach their skin, carve their faces, straighten their hair, and deny their culture to get nearer to it.

Supremacy indicates power, authority, and status. *White supremacy* best describes elevating people based on skin color and physical features as well as the sense of separation and domination involved in the process of whiteness protecting whiteness regardless of the presence or absence of racial hatred. White supremacy occurs at both a collective and an individual level. Goodness and competence are projected onto white people while deviance and incompetence are projected on the other. This gets encoded into institutions and systems. It also becomes internalized and projected. Think of the deluded patient telling everyone he's a doctor versus the actual Black women doctors. Or Henry Louis Gates Jr. arrested in his own home, Oprah refused an item in a store the salesperson deemed too expensive for her (as if), children sent home from school for natural hair, and people all over the world rejecting their facial features, skin tone, hair texture, culture, and very being because they do not conform to what is deemed superior.

While some white people are willing to acknowledge the supremacist aspects of the systems out there, they are less willing to examine the way white supremacy operates within them. White dominance can manifest overtly as not challenging racist comments from relatives or feeling uncomfortable with strong challenges to dominant power. But internalized white supremacy also creeps into attitudes, responses, and assumptions about everyone around us. Who is called on most often in the classroom? Who is assumed to deserve a promotion? What are the starting salaries of your employees based upon (and who even asks for a raise, promotion, or reference)? What are your assumptions about people you pass on the street (and do you even notice these thoughts)?

Although we are not one, we are not separate. And although we are not separate, we are not the same. If we believe the delusion of separation, we will succumb to narratives of domination. And yet if we insist all of us are the same, we can never understand the ways this delusion affects us differently. Depending where we are positioned in the concentric circles, we might not see clearly what is occurring for others. Many of us are taught to not love ourselves, to not belong to ourselves. We are instructed to abandon the margins for a center where aspects (dashikis and dreadlocks) must be abandoned in order to gain entry (but somehow, we are still denied access).

But whether we hate the shape of our nose or the shape of our body, strive to be supremely perfect or supremely productive, reject our culture or reject the margins, we still belong.

No Part Left Out: Self-Love Is All Love

Watching the moon
at midnight,
solitary, mid-sky,
I knew myself completely,
No part left out.

—IZUMI SHIKIBU

Someone just starting as a meditation teacher asked me how I worked with people one-on-one—what was my core philosophy? I thought about it and realized I didn't have much of one except this: *Love 'em up.* I know. That's not a particularly complex methodology. And lest you think I'm a complete fraud, I do give people different suggestions based on their needs. But I find that most of us walk around with a primary wound: thinking there is something wrong with us that needs fixing. Here's a famous quote from Japanese Zen teacher Suzuki Roshi: "All of you are perfect just as you are. And you could use a little improvement." The second sentence sounds like a sly insult, but it's actually an invitation into a deep self-love. It's an opportunity to adore oneself so completely that imperfections are part of the perfection of your being. No part left out. Until we contend with that, our practice is simply a battle with ourselves, a self-evaluation project dressed up as self-acceptance. We turn to practice (or anything) as a way to change ourselves, rejecting love for ourselves because self-love does not jive with our need to improve. I have two primary strategies for deflecting self-love: seeking love from others (often romantically) and, its twisted sister, constant caregiving of others. These tendencies deserve my love too.

In my twenties I was obsessed with boys. What am I talking about?—I've always been and always will be obsessed with boys. It was simply especially pronounced in my twenties. I was looking to be loved by someone else. I was seeking that approval from the outside. Also, I slept around a lot. It was an external validation that I sought based on sexual desirability. If someone desired me sexually that meant that I could love myself. I dressed the part in too-tight clothes (by that I mean: uncomfortable). I longed to belong to someone else's gaze. Hopefully, many people's gazes (more eyes, more love).

And I was still a supernerd. So, even before I went back to grad school to immerse myself in the high theory of cultural studies and postmodernism, I was reading Foucault for fun. I had a series of relationships where the guys I dated did not connect to my intellectualism. Actually, if I mentioned what I was reading, there was often condemnation: *Why do you read that stuff? What's the point of that anyways, it's just mental masturbation.* I sensed the threat elicited by my interest in something they did not understand. I learned to not talk about anything that would threaten their sense of belonging (or their masculinity). When we belong to ourselves, we make room for all our ways of being, but we can't give someone else belonging. We can't even make it easier for someone else to belong. All we can do is belong ourselves. Even when others are demanding we belong to them.

Another pattern of mine is getting pulled into other people's crises and dramas. This one is sneaky. And sly. And devious. And all the other words for seeming like something that it's not. It looks commendable and generous, even selfless. It's not. It's often a pattern adopted from our family dynamics (me, yup). The need to be needed by others is a habit preventing us from fully loving ourselves and feeling loved. As adults, it *is* possible to release those patterns, but it can be harder when they're practiced to the point of being a way of life (yes, talking to myself). My tendency to put other people's needs before mine (especially people in emotional distress) can be triggered in a matter of seconds. The sound of someone's voice on the phone can lead me scrambling to find the right response to fix what's wrong. I often compromise my well-being in the process: staying up with someone when I need sleep, allowing conversations to be dominated by others' issues, sidelining what I want for the sake of someone else's demands. It's not that caring about others is bad. Of course not. But it can easily become the way we try and seek love. Compulsive compassion can become so ingrained that I sometimes spend free time going through lists of friends considering who might need support. This could be coming from kindness, but it also could be coming from a longing to be liked and remembered myself, a need to be seen as caring and generous. It's also a way to avoid deeper issues within me that I am not willing to face, perhaps the need to feel better than others. Only I will know the difference.

Here's the thing: self-love is all love. If we *can* love ourselves fully, we *can* love others but, also, when we *do* love ourselves, we *do* love others. Think about it: if we are not separate, on an absolute, everything-is-energy level, truly caring for ourselves *is* caring for others. I remember an early silent retreat where I understood this: that mindfulness is always imbued with kindness. In a deep sitting meditation, I felt my awareness as a fully present, loving attention to my moment-to-moment experience. And when I turned that attention to the others in the meditation hall, I was filled with deep affection for every person there. True presence is filled with that interested care, with kindness and curiosity. These days, I check in with myself before reaching out or responding, making sure my connection is coming from a place of love. When we are fully aware, the response is always loving—even if this means saying "no."

Inner No-ing

Forgotten toddler tantrums aside, I've never been good at saying "no." People pleasing, compulsive compassion, Wonder Woman-ing, Parker Posey party girling, and exaggerated empathy have long led to cycles of overdrive followed by burnout. These im-balanced ways of reacting to the world are definitely learned behavior. Growing up, I got plenty of messages about being a caretaker and putting others first while also being successful and sexy—Enjoli (look it up, millennials). But I am a grown-ass woman now and am learning to say "no." My friend Maria uses the phrase "*Inner No-ing.*" I say, say "yes" to Inner No-ing. "No" is a complete sentence.

But why is it so hard to say it? And mean it? For me, there are a few things operating (they feed into and on each other):

1. **The need to please.** This one is my kryptonite. I have a voracious need for approval. It's wound up closely with number 2 but is more outwardly focused—it's about the actions I take more than the messages I receive/interpret. In the past, the need to please had me accepting almost every invitation that I received.

2. **Fear of rejection.** It's embarrassing how much positive feedback buoys me and how much criticism cuts. I'm not the only one: I have a friend who remembers nothing of the multiple good reviews written about her artistic project from twenty-plus years ago, but she can quote entire sentences from the one bad review (from a shitty publication). The need to belong is wired into us for survival. And maybe it's been taken a little too far—we will not be eaten by wild animals if we don't go to someone's birthday gathering.

3. **FOMO, aka greed.** "Fear of missing out" is really an acronym for greed. And greed is really a not-so-smart strategy for dealing with the impermanence and unreliability of life. If I distract myself with all the things to do, the things to visit, the things to read/watch/eat/consume, maybe that will keep suffering at bay (um, nope). A smarter strategy is, as Suzuki Roshi describes, "accepting that things go away."

4. **The pull of culture and my own conditioning.** The Buddhist path (or any spiritual practice) is described as "going against the stream." That's how the Buddha described it 2,600 years ago, and there was no social media then. Now

it's like going against the tsunami. It's hard not to be pulled
by the messages of our time, including hyperproductivity
and overwhelm as norms (even badges of pride).

Here are four areas where I am focusing my nos (and they are
also messily interrelated):

1. *No* to obligations—not saying yes to things out of guilt or
   shame.

2. *No* to (the need for) confirmations—not needing approval
   for every decision.

3. *No* to distractions—not allowing my attention to get
   hijacked by the priorities of others.

4. *No* to compulsions—not allowing my decisions to be
   determined by unhealthy habits and patterns.

All of these require me to cultivate awareness and presence,
which requires me to slow down, which require me to create space
and time for meditation or other contemplative practices. "No"
requires pausing. Pausing is a radical "no." As a young adult, I explored transgressive spaces and acts and was exposed to boundary
pushing in every domain. I remember wondering at nineteen or
twenty what (if anything) would seem truly radical once all the
boundaries had been challenged in work and art and sex and life?
Today, the most radical act I can imagine for myself is to love myself with abandon, to indulge in self-care with no sense of guilt or
obligation. No consuming. No constructing. No compulsion. Just
being—followed by a long nap.

Connect Yourself

Aren't We Done Yet?

We have done a *lot* of work on ourselves through these chapters. How much more is there? Aren't we done yet!?

No. Belonging is an ongoing process. And belonging is relational. Because, hello, that's where not belonging started in the first place: in relationship, in *connection*. I must not forget (or try to remember when I do) those places where I still separate, where I need to connect. There's work to be done because there's so much connection that is possible. Grounding, knowing, and loving connect you to yourself. Connecting links you to everything else, which is not always easy because everything else includes other people. Everything else also includes everything.

Let me be clear: by *everything*, I mean every damn thing: all people, animals, other beings, so-called inanimate objects, the sky,

Earth, cosmos . . . also, both the joy and the pain, the brilliant and the mundane, the ecstasy and the horror inherent in all of it. I know, I know. I hear you: *Whoa, that's not possible. How can I merge completely into everything? How can I be in complete connection with the universe all the time?* You're right! It feels impossible. But it is possible to contemplate and comprehend that we are not separate from all of reality.

If nothing is separate, why do I need to connect? Paradox alert! Yes, *connect yourself* is the least accurate "imperative as chapter title" thus far. It implies a disconnection to correct. The subtitle of this book should actually say: *A Call to Remember the Inherent Connection with Everything Within Which You Always Already Exist.* We are always connected. We just need to remember it—and learn to be aware of it. Throughout this book, we have laid the groundwork for feeling more intimacy within ourselves. Now we are ready to feel the matrix of life within which we exist. We can handle that. And when we feel we can't, we can follow the steps to ground, know, and love *so that* we can (re)connect.

For some of us, connection to others can be the most challenging part of belonging. Because of traumas and hurts, we don't trust or maybe don't believe in the possibility of connecting. But all of us have experienced connection, whether we remember it or not. I have a story that my family was not physically connected. And to some extent, it's true. We did not grow into a very physically intimate unit. I don't remember hugs from either of my parents or extended family. But just because I don't remember it clearly, it doesn't mean it didn't happen.

I heard an interview with the author Darnell Moore where he acknowledges that traumas he experienced growing up poor and

Black and gay make him forget how much goodness he did have in his childhood. He was reminded of it by seeing a photo of himself as a kid smiling. When my mom died, my sister-in-law sent me photos of my mother with my two nephews, her only grandchildren. In a series of three photos of her hugging my youngest nephew when he was around the age of six, she displayed a physicality and glee that surprised me. I had no memories of my mom being that way. Then when my aunt Hirut died four months after my mom, my cousin sent me a photo of me and my sister with her. I must have been six, my sister ten, and we are draped around my aunt in the most natural physicality. I have no memory of that moment and, more importantly, of that connection. I had lost that sense memory of the intimate physicality that at one point was so obviously a natural part of my being and of my family's ways.

We are remembering. Remembering what we've forgotten, what's been covered over by complexity. By comparison and competition. By domination and oppression. It's true: we've never not belonged. But, as we've seen through our work thus far, most of us have believed the lie of separation since childhood. Unbelieving it takes some undoing. All the ways we become ungrounded, all the ways we forget who we are, all the ways we stop loving ourselves in every moment . . . those are the ways we have disconnected from our inherent interconnection.

Images of meditators in full lotus position with their eyes closed can lead us to think meditation is only an inner practice. That once we master our personal landscape of sensations and emotions, we are complete. Nope. That central Buddhist discourse on mindfulness, the Satipatthana Sutta, contains a refrain that is repeated over a dozen times—it instructs us *to abide contemplating internally, to abide contemplating externally, and to abide contemplating both internally and externally.* This instruction reminds us that our freedom and joy are dependent on the capacity to balance internal awareness with the external (because it's all interconnected anyways). We are not only aware of ourselves or even only aware of what's not our-selves, we are contemplating our own experience (internally), the experiences outside of us (externally), and we are aware of their connection (both internally and externally).

Embodied awareness, self-knowledge, and self-love are the foundations. When we love ourselves in every moment, we ex-perience the external world through love and can support our own sense of belonging. We can be aware of both our internal and external experiences and experience the connection between the two. How do we do this? You know what I'm going to say by now . . . practice. We can practice reconnecting.

Where to Start? Land, Ancestors, Legacy

I was lucky to spend my elementary school years in a tree-lined neighborhood with yards and access to land. As a child, I was closer to the ground (also because I was shorter). I spent a lot of time exploring in the dirt outside our house: digging for worms, watching slithering slugs after a storm, counting legs on centi-pedes, poking roly-poly potato bugs until they wound themselves into a ball. I climbed on the roof of our garage and picked cherries from the tree that pressed against the tiles, I pulled honeysuckle flowers from the bushes that lined our backyard and sucked the sweet dew from the stamens, I stained my fingers pulling mulberries from the trees that stretched across the alleyway behind our house.

Working with urban teens in my twenties, I was struck by how many of them were terrified by insects. If we happened to be on a field trip to a park where ants, cicadas, or any other creature emerged from the dirt, there were shrieks of terror and no amount of pleading about how they were harmless would calm their upset. Some of us have little connection to what teems underneath the pavement. Some of us have been privileged to connect to pristine land, accessing the abundant beauty of this planet, including its slugs. We have differing levels of access to what we label "nature" (even if it's *all* nature, including us).

Much of contemporary not belonging can be traced to our disconnection from the Earth. At the beginning of the twentieth century, only 15 percent of the world's population lived in urban areas. The United Nations identifies 2007 as the turning point— now more than 50 percent of people live in urban areas and by 2050, it will be closer to 70 percent. It has become a privilege to be connected to land that has not been transformed by modernity, land that has not been covered over by concrete or asphalt, land that has not been augmented for human use only. To land that is still ancestral land.

Whether we have access to undeveloped nature or not, many in the world are living in places ravaged by the domination of separation on stolen and unceded land. Eighty percent of the world has been colonized. And even on land untouched by European coloni-

zation like Thailand, Liberia, and China—or even my homeland
of Ethiopia—empire and patriarchy oppressed indigenous people.
Even in Europe itself, land was taken, languages suppressed, and
cultures wiped out.

Reconnecting ourselves requires understanding where we live
and why. This is not only about enjoying the sunset or the sounds of
the sea (though, by all means, enjoy the sunset or the sea!). Just as
we have been learning not to be in contention with our pasts in our
personal lives, we must also learn to not be in contention with our
collective history. We cannot change the past. Right now, we can
learn (and share) what has happened, remember the legacy of those
that came before us, and acknowledge the land that connects us to
them and their people now. We can honor indigenous land.

"Land acknowledgement" is a formal statement in the documents
of an organization or community or made orally at the beginning of
public events. It names and honors the indigenous people of a place
or territory, particularly in settler colonial countries (places where
the indigenous populations were effectively replaced by invading
people). Land acknowledgment is a common practice in Canada,
New Zealand, and Australia and has been growing recently in the
United States. In Toronto public schools, it is done at the start of
each school day, and even hockey games begin with this practice
across Canada. Honoring native land can be a beautiful, heartfelt
tribute to the truths of our current homes and the stimulus to
learning more about indigenous cultures. Land acknowledgement
can also be a perfunctory utterance that does not convey any understanding of its primary intention.

Belonging involves reckoning with what is. We belong to the
beauty of nature. We also belong to the injustice and harm that

allows us to witness this sunset, on this particular hill, in this particular spot of land that holds a particular history. We may be related to those who lived here for thousands of years, we may not know from which land our ancestors came, or we may know that our ancestors displaced others through violence and brutality. We may have a deep bond with land that carried our ancestors for one decade or many centuries. We may grieve for our ancestors forcibly removed from their original lands. When we take the time to learn about the peoples who inhabited a place for thousands of years, those who stewarded it with care and responsibility, we connect ourselves to a long legacy of belonging that emphasized harmony and balance with nature. As we lament the changes to the natural world that are currently producing disorder and destruction, we can also give thanks for what is still in balance due to indigenous wisdom and compassion handed down through the generations.

Connecting myself starts by learning the names and history of the indigenous peoples of where I live and every place I visit. When I travel anywhere in North America, I use the app Native-Land.ca to understand on whose territory I currently am. I search for information about the history and culture of the people and, when teaching, share what I've learned. I commit to begin every teaching, every vacation, every day with connecting to land, to what is literally supporting my very being in every moment. I give thanks, bringing love and kindness to this place. Living in Brooklyn, I regularly remember and honor the Lenape peoples for their stewardship of my current home. Remember, we are all indigenous to somewhere. Honoring indigeneity allows us to honor what has come before.

My own ancestors exist with me wherever I am. I mean that in a woo-woo way as well as on a modern sciencey-science level. Every single cell in my body connects me to those that came before me. Even if we have no knowledge of our ancestors, they live inside every atom within us in the form of genetic and epigenetic information. I personally believe my ancestors also surround me (hanging out in the eternal energy of this universe). Their all-encompassing presence can be unwelcome information for those of us who have some knowledge of our ancestors and don't like what we know. We carry all of our ancestry in us, and we need to acknowledge and accept this. By acknowledging and accepting them, we can help heal the intergenerational and present traumas of our lineages. All of us have problematic ancestors, those who harmed others because of their own ignorance and conditioning. We do not need to reject these ancestors, rather we call on the ancestral wisdom that will be of most benefit to us. Just as we turn to our wisest friends for advice, when I invoke my lineage by lighting incense or making an offering to my ancestor altar, I create a distinction by calling in the wisest parts of my ancestry. Knowing I carry them and their legacy with me to wherever I am, I honor my history coming together with the places I find myself.

Acknowledging the roots of the spiritual teachings I incorporate in my life and in my work is another important part of connecting myself. I recognize and honor the legacy of Asian lineages that preserved Buddhist teachings for thousands of years. With the growth of mindfulness and meditation, it can be easy for white supremacy (see, it's not so bad) to erase the origins of these practices making us think meditation (yoo-hoo! same thing, yoga) started with white celebrity teachers. Honoring Asian ancestors of Buddhist lineages helps me connect my practice to its indigenous roots. Whenever I teach, I follow a land acknowledgement with an honoring of Asian lineages and, if there's time, an invitation for participants to share with each other where their people are from.

Indigenous land, my indigeneity, and the indigeneity of my practice all come together. I begin to connect myself right here.

It's Elemental: We Are Nature

Listen to the air. You can hear it, feel it, smell it, taste it. Woniya wakan—the holy air—which renews all by its breath. Woniya, woniya wakan—spirit, life, breath, renewal—it means all that. Woniya—we sit together, don't touch, but something is there; we feel it between us, as a presence. A good way to start thinking about nature, talk about it. Rather, talk to it, talk to the rivers, to the lakes, to the winds as to our relatives.

—JOHN FIRE LAME DEER
(MINECONJU-LAKOTA SIOUX)

Many of us long to connect to nature as if nature exists somewhere else. Out there, in the countryside or on a mountain top. Nature lives at the beach, or maybe in the park. Not here on the grimy sidewalk or on a busy subway. Here's the deal: We are nature. This entire giant ball of aliveness hurtling through space (you know, Earth), *this* is nature. The space itself—nature. All we can see and not see, feel and not feel: all nature. And we are all connected to it.

A very simple classical mindfulness practice can help us remember that connection. The simple part can be a barrier in this case. It's a formal practice—right there in the same section of the Satipatthana Sutta as the breath and body meditations, given the same importance as mindfulness of thoughts and emotions—yet most modern mindfulness teachers rarely teach this practice. Modernity trained us to be impressed by the complex metaphors of science, but this practice is so simple, people can dismiss it as simplistic. It instructs us to bring awareness to the elements of earth, water, fire, and air. That's it. Four things. Not the one hundred and eighteen elements of high school chemistry (my worst subject). Just four simple elements. Simple, but not simplistic.

I was on retreat recently and began a list of all the things I do not know about the world. I don't know how my digestion works, I don't know the names of clouds, I don't know how planes fly, I don't know how (or why) my hair is turning gray, I don't know why birds make formations at certain times and not others, I don't know how most mechanical or electronic things work, I don't know how acorns become trees. The number of things I don't know are endless. But I can know the experience of these four elements as a way to connect to absolutely all the things I claim not to know. These four categories can be applied to absolutely everything around us. Connecting to them within our own bodies allows us to connect to them in the world.

The classical elements are referred to in the ancient traditions of almost every continent—from ancient Egypt and Greece to China and India to the indigenous traditions of Africa and the Americas. You can think of the elements as basic categories for natural experience. In the classical mindfulness teachings of Buddhism, we use the four elements of earth, fire, water, and air as objects for contemplation in the same way we use the breath as an object. Meditation on the elements helps connect us to our bodies in a way that also connects us to everything else in nature. I find that for the purposes of connection, four is a perfect amount of experiences to keep track of internally, externally, and both internally and externally.

Earth is solidity, the mass within us (bones, cartilage, teeth, flesh) corresponding to all that is solid in the world including soil, trees, plants, rocks, and other animals. The weight of your body sitting can be experienced as the earth element. This element feels heavy and dense. The stability of the land beneath you helps you feel grounded and rooted, like a tree. Your bones and flesh—all that is solid and dense in the body—are earth in you.

Water signifies liquid, moisture, and fluidity in the body (blood, saliva, gurgling) and represents all the manifestations of water, whether liquid, solid, or gaseous. Water feels smooth and flowing. Water is often associated with the realm of emotions and all our feelings. Our body is about 60 percent water, and this element makes up most of our planet, too. Water is life.

Fire refers to our temperature (heat, coldness), epitomized by the hotness of the sun. Fire is energy; it burns and transmutes. It is connected to our ability to take action and effect change. Wherever you feel warm or cool—your face, your back, your armpits, your hands, anywhere on your skin or inside you—this is the fire element in you. You might notice this change within and around you throughout the day as the weather shifts (and notice your various responses to the changes).

Air is any wind in the body (breath, gas) and surrounds us throughout our atmosphere. Air feels movable and changeable, light and ephemeral. Air is connected to the mental realm of thoughts. Of course, in our bodies the air element is exemplified by the breath. By bringing awareness to your breath, you can bring the air element in the body into connection with the air that surrounds and connects us all.

Some people find this meditation challenging; it seems abstract. It can be helpful to think of the elements as metaphors. Metaphors simplify what seems complex so that we can relate to it better. Here's another way to think of it: *Although the elements are not one, they are not separate. And although they are not separate, they are not the same.* A tree grows as the earth element supported by the water from rain, the carbon dioxide of air, and the fire of the sun. When it is cut and burned for warmth it transmutes into the fire element and releases to the air, its moisture evaporated away by the heat, its ashes returned to the earth to nourish the next generation of growth. We may know intellectually that we are connected to everything around us and that we originate from the exact same substance as all of our known reality; it's true, we are stardust. But the seeming complexity of life—all the names and classifications, all the species and categories, designations, and intricacies—can be overwhelming. Meditating on the elements helps connect us to everything else in nature. We are nature, too. Experiencing these elements as a felt sense connects us to this truth.

Feeling the elements can take time. There will be a practice at the end of this book to help you connect to them. For now, consider if there's any part of your experience that cannot be classified into these elements. It may be helpful to know that in many traditions there exists a fifth element of ether or spirit to account for what seems mysterious. Everything else in our experience is at least one of these four: solid, fluctuating in temperature, fluid, or ephemeral—our bodies, emotions, actions, and thoughts. What else exists? Not much, right? If we simply observe our experience, we can use these four words to name every single experience we encounter within and outside of us.

In fact, these elements help us relate the inside to the outside. Saying "air, air, air" as I witness this breath enter and leave the body allows me to contemplate what transpires both internally and externally. Feeling the solidity of my own body in contact with the solidity of the chair underneath me right now as I silently consider "earth" enables me to connect with what often seems separate. As my extremities cool with the lowering temperature, I recognize that "fire" includes the constant fluctuations of the climate. And as I blink at this screen, I feel the moistness in my eyes, recognizing that "water" is constantly evaporating and condensing into various forms internally and externally. I experience the water element when I fill the kettle, fire when I light the stove, air when I open a window to feel the breeze, and earth in the wood floor beneath my feet. When I feel especially *airy*, I can emphasize the groundedness of earth. When I I feel too *firey*, I can encourage the moistness of water. Parts of me (my breath, skin cells, heat, and tears) continually mix and meld with the rest of nature. I am nature. I belong to it all.

Synchronicity:
The Inescapable Network of Mutuality

Belonging denotes relationship. As we explore belonging deeply, we discover that we are inextricably intertwined with what is ostensibly outside of us. The elements help us on an experiential, felt sense level recognize our interconnection with all matter and space around us. For better or worse, all matter and space includes other people, and this can be witnessed through many processes of the body.

Mirror neurons were discovered by Italian neurophysiologists in the 1990s. They were studying the neural activity of monkeys, including monitoring the area of the brain that controls motor activity. One day a researcher reached for his own food while in the lab and noticed neurons begin to fire in the monkeys' premotor cortexes—the same area that showed activity when the animals made a similar hand movement. The monkeys were sitting still and merely watching him, but their brains exhibited mirror activity, as if they were performing the action themselves. This research radically altered the way we think about ourselves. Scientists believe it explains why we flinch when we see a stranger slam their finger in a door or why we scrunch up our face when we watch someone eating a lemon. We instinctively and immediately understand each other's experience on a felt sense level, as if we are experiencing it ourselves. Mirror neurons are so complex that our brains distinguish between someone grabbing a cup and their intention behind that action: if we see someone grasp a cup to drink, our mirror neurons will code that differently than someone's grasp to clear the cup from a table. We are not just simulating another person's actions, but also the intentions and emotions behind those actions. Before this discovery, we considered our brains to be logical thought process machines that *know* the things of the world. Now, many have come to believe that we understand our world largely through *feeling*, not thinking. If you see someone laugh, your neurons will mirror a laugh, creating the feelings associated with laughing within you.

And it's not only inside our brains where our connection with each other is wired. Multiple research studies show that our heartbeats also synchronize with others', even strangers'. When not synced, people have different heart rates and rhythms with little relationship to each other, but heart rates will sync up quite easily. For people who are connected, like lovers, it happens simply by sitting in the same room. It also occurs between two strangers who are asked to perform a task together, people in a choir singing, and even an audience of strangers watching a live theater performance. It seems that shared experience overcomes perceived differences to produce profound physiological connection.

Whether we have a large network of friends and family or mostly only socialize with one pet and one bestie, we are connected. But sometimes we need to practice *feeling* connected. Whenever I lead a relational exercise inviting people to share their experiences with each other, I give the instruction to listen deeply to the other person. I explain that often, when someone else is speaking, we are not fully engaged. Rather than giving them our full attention, we may be thinking about something else, judging what they are saying, or simply waiting for our turn to speak. Often, we are planning our own words and miss what the other person has to offer. Especially, if we have not done the work of loving ourselves fully, we will be preoccupied with worries about ourselves (*How am I measuring up?*) and miss the presence and power of the other person. If we are emotionally distressed in any way, we're even less available to sync with others. And this, too, is an opening to belonging.

Remember, social pain feels just like physical pain. We evolved physical pain to warn us of danger; perhaps the same is true for social pain, too. The late neuroscientist John Cacioppo believed we evolved to experience loneliness because it can be useful, even though it's so unpleasant. Humans have survived through forming cooperative groups. If people feel they are excluded from a group, then feelings of loneliness might drive them to connect with people, find new friends, or rekindle old relationships.

We are wired to connect to others. We evolved to sync up with those around us, to feel what they feel. It's almost as if our bodies, knowing our inherent interconnection, long to remind us of our synchronicity. We don't have to do anything particularly special to experience this interconnection: simply pay attention and feel. *Be longing.* Even in isolation, our feelings will lead us to the truth of belonging.

There is an elaborate network of relationships that make up even the most simple life. Here's how Martin Luther King Jr. described it over fifty years ago:

It really boils down to this: that all life is interrelated.
We are all caught in an inescapable network of mutuality,
tied into a single garment of destiny. Whatever affects one
directly, affects all indirectly. We are made to live together

because of the interrelated structure of reality. Did you ever stop to think that you can't leave for your job in the morning without being dependent on most of the world? You get up in the morning and go to the bathroom and reach over for the sponge, and that's handed to you by a Pacific Islander. You reach for a bar of soap, and that's given to you at the hands of a Frenchman. And then you go into the kitchen to drink your coffee for the morning, and that's poured into your cup by a South American. And maybe you want tea: that's poured into your cup by a Chinese. Or maybe you're desirous of having cocoa for breakfast, and that's poured into your cup by a West African. And then you reach over for your toast, and that's given to you at the hands of an English-speaking farmer, not to mention the baker. And before you finish eating breakfast in the morning, you've depended on more than half the world. This is the way our universe is structured, this is its interrelated quality. We aren't going to have peace on Earth until we recognize this basic fact of the interrelated structure of all reality.

Arguably, life across this globe is even more interconnected now than in 1967. Not on an absolute level of course—it's just as non-separate as it was then. But on a relative level? Oh yes. Human migration has increased so much that there are as many as eight hundred languages spoken in New York City. We are connected by an immense communication network (including the connectors we carry around in our pockets). And yet, on average, people in

Western society feel more disconnected than ever . . . thwarted by modernity's lack of community.

Connection and Community

I have never been able to regard [isolation] as anything but the result of separation. Time has not changed my point of view, nor has the knowledge that what separates people are not the dreary marginal issues of race, class, or gender, but this: those who believe friendship and love dispel our basic aloneness, and those who do not.

——HILTON ALS, *THE WOMEN*

Scientists have recognized for decades that strong emotional bonds within a community protect people from illness and help them live longer. Known as the Roseto Effect, the name refers to a homogenous Italian American community in mid-1960s Roseto, PA. The research showed that this close-knit community reported remarkably lower rates of heart disease than neighboring towns. But these were not "Mediterranean diet" Italians: they engaged in heavy smoking, drinking, and eating (lots of meatballs and sausages fried in lard). Their superior health is attributed solely to their community's cohesiveness and lack of stress. With very little hierarchy, everyone lived more or less alike. Over the years, as the cohesiveness disappeared, the mortality rates in Roseto increased.

For decades, cardiovascular disease and cancer rates were considerably higher in industrialized countries. While there were higher opportunistic and infectious disease deaths, chronic or noncommunicable (i.e., stress-related) diseases were less common in the global south until very recently. I don't know of any research that links the Roseto Effect to colonization and development. I do know my family lost its cohesiveness with migration. Ethiopian and Eritrean cultures, like most traditional societies of the global south, are built on community and connection. My parents grew up in very different circumstances from each other—my mother in the capital of Ethiopia (Addis Ababa), my father in a small rural village in Eritrea. My mother was a city girl who adored Omar Sharif while my father herded goats as a kid. By the sixties and seventies, Ethiopia was modernizing, and both of my parents were of the generation that dressed in what they called European clothing (though their parents did not) and worked in modernizing offices. They occasionally ate pasta or pizza, but their lives were primarily woven into the ancient rhythm of family, community, food, and customs. The religious culture of saint's days, fasting, and seasonal celebrations shaped their calendar. They each grew up in large families (seven and eight kids respectively) within a network of extended members. Grandparents and great aunts and uncles lived in the home or nearby. Cousins were often raised like siblings. When we moved to DC, my family took in kids of those cousins as well as my own first cousins (all called simply "cousins"); they and a few of my uncles and aunts lived with us for years at a time (another thing that made us different from our white neighbors—relatives living in the basement). We did not have a huge home, so we learned to live in close connection.

Even though we were many people living in our house in DC and my parents surrounded themselves with old and new friends from back home, we could never approximate what was left behind. And as the Roseto studies show, even communities that tried to replicate the belonging of tradition—staying close together, planting gardens with familiar herbs, maintaining cultural songs and dances, passing down old tales and stories—eventually lost their cohesiveness. Children desire to be more like what they see around them, begin to adopt mainstream ways, enter a competitive workforce, move away, and maybe marry someone from a different culture.

Remember: it was not the homogeneity that kept people healthy, it was the connection as well as lack of stress and absence of intense hierarchy and oppression within the group. We can't overly romanticize "traditional culture"—there are problems and inequities that exist in every society, and homogeneity can bring its own challenges (like the constrictions of conformity). There are many benefits to the multiculturalism brought by migration. But with migration, the dissolution of traditional communities has happened over and over again for various ethnic groups. In addition, we have people, including African Americans and the indigenous people of the Americas (and wherever settler colonialism exists) whose community and connection were forcibly stolen from them. Many immigrants themselves come from lands where violence and cultural theft perpetrated on them also destroyed community.

It is still possible (and necessary) for our well-being to belong within community and culture. Some traditional communities still survive with cohesiveness and interconnection today. There are immigrant groups and enclaves that foster and protect a tight-knit network, discouraging assimilation and intermarriage. That's one way. Many of us (me included) attempt to cultivate a sense of interconnection and belonging across various groups of people, honoring the multiplicity of our cultural realities, even if those multiplicities can sometimes be utterly confounding. Being in multiple cross-cultural relationships means understanding and relating to many ways of being. This gives us the opportunity to interact with awareness and to remember we are connected to everything, even the most unexpected.

So Many Rules!

The people of Roseto lost their cohesiveness as they melted into the pot of larger American culture. Today more and more of us are making up rules as we go along. In many ways this benefits us. We learn from different people and abandon outdated, oppressive, and unquestioned ways of the past. But a tight-knit community or a larger homogenous society often has clearer rules. Remember, the Roseto Effect is credited solely to interconnection. Italian immigrants who stuck together had not yet dispersed into the larger American culture like the Irish and Welsh communities in neighboring towns. Even though the men of Roseto worked in similar danger-ous mining jobs, even though as the newest immigrants (not yet absorbed into whiteness) they experienced a lot of discrimination, even though many in the community experienced poverty, their health was vastly better.

These people lived very modest, close-knit lives with three gen-erations in every household and virtually no social stratification between those with differing incomes. Cohesiveness like this can create a low-stress environment. Cohesiveness also comes with conformity. Conformity provides structure. Everyone more or less believes the same thing, and life is lived according to a prede-termined schedule and rhythm. Work, meals, holidays, and rites of passage are all experienced according to long-held traditions: grace is said at the start of a meal, community gathers to help celebrate or mourn, obligations are kept to elders and to the ill, and everyone knows the rules. Conformity can also breed intolerance. People with differing opinions, orientations, and identities can be marginalized or even punished, harmed, or killed.

Many of us don't feel a sense of deep connection to any one culture or community. As a young person, I experienced not belonging as a constant sense that I was breaking the rules of one culture or another. My parents were already mixing cultures in Ethiopia. My family further diluted our rules when we emigrated. When we moved here, Amharic was my only language. I started to learn English in preschool. By the age of five, I refused to speak my native tongue and my parents, not wanting to upset my integration into our new home, complied. They continued to speak to me in our language and I would answer in English. Over the years, I lost fluency and regressed to my baby Amharic. I understand only basic conversation. And, as I mentioned, I cannot read or write in our alphabet at all.

My parents did not limit us to our traditional culture. How could they? They didn't limit themselves. But there were also mixed messages. I was not allowed to play soccer, but my mom also did not want me stuck in the kitchen so she never taught me to cook (my husband makes a better *misir wot* than I do—she taught him). They were doing the best they could as they navigated what it means to cross borders and blend cultures. They must have thought, even unconsciously, that keeping us away from our traditions—or at least not forcing them on us—was the best thing for us to assimilate and succeed. These days there are more and more young Ethiopians and Eritreans who don't speak their traditional languages, but hardly anyone I meet my age is as nonfluent and illiterate as I am. Sometimes I meet people of my generation who are angry with my lack of fluency, as if I intentionally won't speak Amharic (oh, yeah, I love being cut off from my culture and feeling rootless).

It's not that I didn't learn from my culture. Here are just a few things that were ingrained in me: fight to pay the check (push, pull, sneak a card to the waiter, even almost storm out of the restaurant in a dramatic fit to get your way); when you call someone, ask at least fifteen times how they are (and barely let them answer as you repeat the inquiry even before letting them know who you are); tend to the elders first (my twist: ignore the part about tending to male elders first); when someone visits, don't take their refusal of food and drink at face value (offer at least four or five times, insisting until they relent to taking something). Cultures clash. Some rules differ from mainstream American rules. Or from the rules of my European husband.

One time, my mom's friend came over. I was tending to something and asked my husband to ask Salome if she wanted something to drink. When I finally got back to the living room, I saw she did not have a beverage. I pulled Frederic aside and asked if he had offered our guest something, to which he replied, "She said she didn't want anything." I realized what might have transpired and inquired, "But how many times did you ask her?" My friend Sarita named this dynamic when describing a similar misunderstanding between an Indian couple and their new American neighbors. When the Indians are visiting and the Americans only offer something once, the visitors go thirsty and hungry (like Salome would have without my intervention). When the Americans visit the Indians, they end up uncomfortably stuffing themselves because rather than consistently refusing, they (confoundingly to the hosts) say yes to every offer of food and drink. What's polite in one culture makes no sense in another. You don't need to be an immigrant or living in a foreign country to experience culture clash. We cross cultures and navigate new rules all the time.

Rules get internalized and become unconscious norms and habits. Since childhood I have chafed against the patriarchal norms of traditional Ethiopian culture, Buddhist traditions, and modern American life. In Ethiopia and Eritrea, guests are expected to be served first, but visiting my cousin's home in Asmara, his domestic worker adamantly refused to start with me even though I was the only visiting guest. She found it impossible to deviate from the men-first rule. In the Thai Forest tradition of Buddhism, to which many of my teachers are connected, female monastics are considered junior to male monastics: nuns are inferior to monks. Yes, that is a crazy sentence to be writing in 2020. There are literal rules encoding this hierarchy. And people (whom I know and love) still study with the monks who enforce this discrimination. This is blamed on arcane rules to which they are somehow grudgingly bound. Sometimes I wonder if we replaced the words "nuns" and "monks" with "Black people" and "white people," would we still consider studying (or even tolerating) those same teachers and teachings? And, each of us must look deep within to see the ways "rules" become habits. (White) women won the right to vote in the US only one century ago. Women here still make less for the same work, are underrepresented in power, and are undervalued almost everywhere. I witness the effects of these rules in myself. Even with all my academic and personal study and practice of feminism, I see the ways I privilege male knowledge and power, the ways I look up to men in power more than women. In turn, unless the subject is race and he is white, I am often dismissed as an authority when paired with a male teacher: inevitably, he will be asked more questions, garner more eye contact, and sometimes what I have stated will later be ascribed to him.

Whenever I lead interactive workshops, we establish agreements of communication and interaction before we begin. This acknowledges that because we come from different cultures and communities, we do not necessarily share values (i.e., rules). It lays a foundation for more meaningful connections and recognizes that our habits have been conditioned by society. One example: those who tend to speak less are invited to step up, those who traditionally speak more are invited to step back. Gender, race, class, and other factors are acknowledged as influencing how we show up (and how we are received). This helps expand our awareness of what occurs in connection. One distinction made is the difference between intent and impact—even when our intentions are those of belonging and non-harming, our personal values and perspectives may clash with those of others and lead to harm. As a group, we agree to consciously avoid harm as well as acknowledge and understand when we have unintentionally cased harm.

Navigating different rules is an ongoing practice in the world-including within both personal and professional spaces. Belonging asks us to connect with all types of people. We should not assume that rules are the same wherever we go. Those of us who have been traveling the concentric circles from the margin to center (and out again) are familiar with how rules are constantly changing, internally and externally. As cultures mix and meld, complexity and confusion can arise. Exploring the complexities of cultural connection is a responsibility of belonging.

Cultures Mix:
Appropriation, Dismissal,
Exchange, and Appreciation

Many white spiritual spaces are cultivated as if there is no culture attached. Places that offer meditation, Reiki, yoga, breathwork, and other powerful techniques present these modalities as if they are expressed neutrally, but there is almost always an unnamed (usually unseen) dominant culture infusing the offerings. The way information is conveyed, the references made, the books/music/media on hand, even the cadence of the speech is laden with culture and bias. Typically, white culture and supremacy. And there are also often appropriated cultures underlying what is on offer. Lineages go unnamed, differences are ignored, and dynamics of power and domination are left unchecked. I have witnessed this happening in my own spiritual communities for years.

Cultures mix. That's the nature of life. Whether or not that mixing is done with attention to the realities of colonization and domination, history and lineage is up to us. My friend Brian and I teach a course about the cultural complexities within Western Buddhism. In it we identify four ways through which cultures can mix: appropriation, dismissal, exchange, or appreciation. The first two involve processes that stay closer to the inner circles without awareness or attention to what is happening at the margins. The latter two involve or engage with the experiences and perspectives of those at the margins with awareness, humility, and respect.

There has been increasing attention given to cultural appropriation, especially every year around the end of October. Halloween seems to bring an annual conversation about why white women should not dress up as Pocahontas or geishas or Arabian princesses (or the sexy version of any of these) or why it was wrong for that frat bro to don blackface. When I say "appropriation," I mean "misappropriation." Cultural appropriation involves instances of people from a dominant culture using objects, practices, or ideas from a nondominant culture inappropriately and/or without acknowledgment or understanding. "Dominant" and "nondominant" are the key words here. This is not the same as a white person invited to wear a sari to the wedding of an Indian friend. Appropriation means someone's native dress is not a "costume" for you to wear for entertainment. And it's never okay to do Black/brownface (. . . Mr. Trudeau). Cultural appropriation can also include the monetization of ideas or objects like the long-standing unacknowledged appropriation of Black blues music by white rock-and-roll musicians. Or how Buddha images and Hindu deities adorn every sort of business or t-shirt without any attention to their intended sacredness. Cultural narratives are consumed by capitalism and the decorating or fashion whims of those who know nothing about indigenous wisdom. But cultural appropriation does not mean we need to completely expunge everything that does not come from our direct lineages.

Sometimes, at the other extreme from appropriation, is cultural dismissal. We see this a lot in the modern mindfulness movement. Cultural dismissal includes the tendency to discount anything that does not meet Western standards of scientific proof. It's the belief that only "others" believe—and the inability to acknowledge the cultural dominance inherent in that assumption. Those who believe in the supernatural *believe*; those who believe in the *New York Times know*. Cultural dismissal is the almost allergic reaction to things that don't fit a model of rationality and reason or dominant styles or tastes. The mysterious or unexplainable gets discounted. Things that look or smell different are rejected. Mysticism is deemed backwards; traditional remedies are labeled bunk. Cultural dismissal begat the word "woo-woo" and perpetuates an arrogant conviction that contemporary Western (i.e., white) approaches are more valid because they have dropped the "cultural baggage" of the past.

Cultural exchange acknowledges the movement of people, ideas, teachings, and objects across different cultures over time. It's why we have the various lineages within Buddhism. The Buddha was born in what is now Nepal, he taught across the Indian subcontinent, his teachings spread throughout Southeast Asia and to Tibet, China, Korea, and Japan. In each place, the ideas, images, and practices morphed and combined with the local traditions. In China they integrated with Taoist and Confucianist ideas, in Tibet they incorporated indigenous Bon spirituality, and in Japan, Shinto customs and practices infused Zen. I witness how postmodern, postcolonial, and feminist theory influence the way I interpret the teachings of the Buddha. I integrate these ideas in conversation with friends and colleagues who challenge my assumptions and take me to task for mistakes I may be making in the process.

Finally, cultural appreciation is the respect given to the traditions of others. I can appreciate another spiritual tradition without adopting it. I can participate in a cultural experience without espousing it. Cultural appreciation is our capacity to acknowledge and honor another person's lineage without the need to appropriate, dismiss, or exchange it.

Learning to listen (and hear) the experiences of others is key to connection, to belonging. Yes, it can be challenging to navigate all the multiplicities and complexities of modern identities. Connecting is the test of belonging. Our wounds around belonging happened relationally. They'll heal that way, too. We all carry unconscious conditioning that, if left unexamined, can impede our connection with others. Making space for practice helps us in connection.

The Haiku Attitude: To Be Touched, to Connect

Peacebuilder and poet John Paul Lederach came to haiku after experiencing burnout from his international work. He experienced writing this form of poetry as a contemplative practice imbued with what he calls the "haiku attitude"—a state of mind that is prepared "to be touched by beauty." When I first heard this phrase, I was struck by the beauty part. Being an aesthete, I was drawn to the idea that I could be touched by what is lovely. I love beauty! I love being connected to pretty things.

I am on yet another long retreat and struggling (a theme of my long retreats). Our usual strategy for any kind of discomfort is to move away from it, discredit it, or get rid of it. If I'm bored or anxious, I find something to distract me. If I don't like something you say, I condemn it. If I don't like something I see, I shut my eyes. But on retreat there's nowhere to go, no one to blame, and your eyes are already shut. As I grapple with sitting practice on this retreat, I remember the poetic guideline to be touched by beauty and take refuge in the glory all around me—wildflowers, dragonflies, bees, chipmunks. I allow myself to connect to summer's beauty. Being connected to nature is good, right?

Well, sort of. As I reflect on the whole phrase, I realize I am emphasizing the wrong part. It's not beauty that's the point, it's the capacity to be touched. Summer's beauty is glorious. And anything, when used to avoid an experience, diminishes our capacity to connect. So, I ration my chipmunk intake, return to the cushion, and allow myself to be touched. And there, I witness things I had not wanted to feel—pain, fear, loss, grief. I meet them with curiosity and kindness and the intention to give them as much time as needed. Without curiosity, I am unable to touch into my sensations and feelings. Without kindness, I cannot feel my fear and pain with spaciousness and patience.

In time, the stillness I had strived for in the beginning as a way to get away from the anxiety and agitation appears as the spacious awareness holding it all. Awareness holding the tension, pain, and fear. Awareness holding the ease, joy, and love. And all of it is beauty. After a few minutes, I hear the bell, and a sense of relief melts the tension of this upright posture. Why do I bring so much rigidity to sitting? I relax my back and stretch it in different directions as I open my eyes to the dim room. Someone has closed all the blinds again. The room is a spacious and stark container. It's not unpleasant, but I see that the clouds have cleared and a longing to be out in the sun fills me. I stay in the still, cool meditation hall until everyone has left but those frozen in their stillness. I untangle my legs and leave the hall, bowing to the Buddha on the main altar and then bowing to the Kuan Yin relegated to the entryway.

As I exit the door to the outside, my senses are awakened. I smell the cut grass like a blast of green. Immediately my skin is warming and my ears are buzzing with the sound of birds. The whirring of a dragonfly passes on my right. The insects have a secret highway system, intricate and invisible (air). I remind myself to reconnect to my body, resting my awareness on my bare feet stepping onto the grass (earth). The dew from this morning has dried (water), and the grass tickles my feet in alternating cool and warm caresses as one foot steps in a path of sunlight while the other moves with the shade (fire). I walk slowly to my favorite path, stopping periodically to observe the life around me. I smile. I breathe in. I sigh audibly. Here, in this moment, I am touched by beauty. I am connected.

Disconnect to Connect: Be the Mystery

On retreat, we disconnect to connect. But not all of us can afford the time or resources to go away for a weekend or week, let alone for months. Yet none of us can afford to *not* make space for space in our lives. We must slow down, pause, and be present in order to access our capacity to truly connect. True connection is not the compulsive compassion of reaching out to someone because we can't tolerate not being needed. True connection involves grounding, knowing, and loving ourselves so that we connect to others from there. We must continually recommit to the silence and space needed for this kind of connection. This takes commitment because silence has become a commodity:

> Silence is now offered as a luxury good. In the business-class lounge at Charles de Gaulle Airport, I heard only the occasional tinkling of a spoon against china. I saw no advertisements on the walls. This silence, more than any other feature, is what makes it feel genuinely luxurious.

When you step inside and the automatic doors whoosh shut behind you, the difference is nearly tactile, like slipping out of haircloth into satin. Your brow unfurrows, your neck muscles relax; after twenty minutes you no longer feel exhausted. Outside, in the peon section, is the usual airport cacophony. Because we have allowed our attention to be monetized, if you want yours back you're going to have to pay for it.

It's true that most of us cannot afford the silence of elite spaces. But how much do we get caught in the noise of the world as our own patterning? Making space for ourselves is possible if we prioritize its importance, if we don't get trapped in constantly doing. When I first heard the phrase "the pathology of productivity" from coach Chela Davison, I recognized in it the anxious fuel for so much in my life. I can still get caught in the loops of grasping connected to worrying, changing, solving, fixing, planning, getting, achieving, attaining. . . . Even after weeks of quarantining, there is still the impulse of doing. If I think everything out, every moment of the day—if I am constantly doing—everything will finally be okay. Besides being impossible, it prevents true connection.

Some years ago, on Thanksgiving Day, I was teaching a retreat at Spirit Rock Meditation Center in California and reflecting on my tendency for constant doing (once again) and recognizing its effect of disconnection. The first peoples of the San Geronimo Valley, where Spirit Rock is located, lived in peaceful communities interdependent with the rest of the natural world around them. Their descendants are known as the Miwok people. The Miwok ancestors fished, hunted, gathered roots and herbs, collected acorns and mushrooms, and in communication with other tribes took care to conserve the wellness of all beings. They "worked" three to four hours per day and spent the majority of their time in creativity, prayer, play, ceremony, and storytelling. Their conflicts were solved through council and consensus, sometimes taking hours and days of discussion and understanding. They did not believe themselves to be separate from each other or anything around, above, or below them.

Whenever I pause and allow myself to reconnect deeply to my heart-mind-body, I can also remember the truth of interconnection. But this requires an intentional, sustained pause—something we all seem less and less capable to allow. Being at Spirit Rock, amid the eucalyptus in the woods and the hawks in the sky (and away from the demands of constant communication and activity), gave easier access to this presence, but even in the busy city, all we need to do is slow down, stop, and look up or down between the cracks of the skyline or the sidewalks and meet the wonder that awaits us. Nature is here, too. Internally and externally.

But presence and deep listening are shadowed by productivity. They're even dismissed by some as passive, useless, unproductive. Presence is overrun by activity and overdoing. Meditation is marketed these days as a cure for stress and anxiety and other ailments . . . so we can *do* more. Sure, it can be that. However, the true power of meditation practice is the radical liberation of our capacity to *be*. And thereby belong. We disconnect to connect to it all, including the mystery. Eugene Gendlin describes it as our capacity to feel the whole universe:

When I use the word "body," I mean more than the physical machine. Not only do you physically live the circumstances around you but also those you only think of in your mind. Your physically felt body is in fact part of a gigantic system of here and other places, now and other times, you and other people—in fact, the whole universe. This sense of being bodily alive in a vast system is the body as it is felt from inside.

Our longing for safety and for what's comfortable is very deep; it's hardwired into us. To let go of the usual discursive focus and simply listen—that's not easy. But our practice is all about that, isn't it? We can be open and curious about emotions, thoughts, and sensations that are moving through us. We cultivate a trust with whatever is arising. Not pin down, not know, not fix. To just be with what's happening. Only then can we open to what is mysterious and unknowable.

Mystery by its very nature is puzzling. It asks us to give up our usual ways of understanding. It asks us to give up control (like we ever had a choice). It insists that we allow for paradoxes. It exists outside language. It presents us with uncertainty and unreliability. It reveals impermanence. Not things we like very much. So we try to push away not-knowing with facts and statistics. We try to hold on to certainty (of happiness, of pleasure, of safety, of solidity, of continuity). We get caught in patterns of comparison and competition and dominance and oppression. We grasp and cling—which creates more suffering.

Belonging is an undoing of this. Ultimately, we don't have to (in fact can't) *do* anything to belong. We can only *be*.

7

Be Yourself

Value Being You

You can't stop the waves, but you can learn to surf.
—SWAMI SATCHIDANANDA

The final imperative of our work together: *Be yourself.*

Simply be. There's nothing to do. No one to compare to. Nowhere to go. Not a thing to achieve. No other possibility but yours. All you can do is be you. What other option is there? Given all the causes and conditions (evolutionary, historical, intergenerational, cultural, familial, personal), given the moment-by-moment occurrences of your life until this very instance right now reading these words—how you are is exactly as you should be. How could you be anything else?

You are perfect just as you are.

(Wait for it.)

And you could use a little improvement.

This is the paradox of the spiritual path. We continually deepen our exploration, integrate our understanding, and evolve our capacities while also resting in the freedom and ease of accepting exactly how things are for us right now. We float along in calm waters, surfing waves that come our way, connecting with the ocean. We do our best by simply being ourselves.

Be ourselves and we belong.

That is, until we find ourselves (once again) questioning our choices, our abilities, our worthiness, our belonging . . . fearing what lurks in the depths, struggling in rough waters, getting pulled under, scrambling to find any safe shore to ride out the storm.

Rudders help.

At the core of the Buddhist path are ethical teachings. At the core of *any* worthwhile wisdom tradition are ethical teachings. Some of us may have received clear principled guidance (spiritual or secular) from our families and communities. But generally, ethics are rarely explored in modern life outside of professional codes and religious communities. Integrity is the foundation for healthy individuals and society; without it, mayhem ensues (this could explain a lot). Without clarity, many of us simply intuit values from various personal and public groups (this also explains things). I don't remember ethics distinctly being taught or discussed in my childhood until I took an elective peace studies class senior year of high school, and that's because I went to a kooky alternative private school.

When I first met Frederic, I was telling an older Buddhist friend that I was in love. She asked me only one question: *Do you share the same values?* I had never before consciously considered that as *the* central question for a relationship. I'd always emphasized similar interests and related communities as crucial. But without the support of shared values, most of us are left to steer the choppy waters of contemporary complexity without any ballast. Our internal contradictions inevitably confuse us, and conflicts arise with others because of differing perspectives. Disagreements occur over money, politics, sexual mores, and food choices. Unconscious biases are left unexamined while patterns of domination play out unintentionally. Public spaces are free-for-alls: bullying is normalized, trolling is tolerated, and gossip is expected.

The five precepts of ethical living in Buddhism serve as a guidance system for my being. Without them, I am at the mercy of the movement of societal waves (and whims). Even with them, I am challenged to explore their changing meaning in my life given my continual personal evolution. At their most simple they demand the following:

1. Don't kill.

2. Don't steal.

3. Don't misuse sexuality.

4. Don't lie.

5. Don't get intoxicated.

I have "broken" all of these many times over. If they're approached as rules, they seem impossible to meet and are mostly unhelpful. I believe we can understand ethical principles in ways that are more supportive. A version of the five precepts written by Caitriona Reed, a Zen teacher and cofounder of Manzanita Village, beautifully interprets them as guidelines for acknowledging the history and context of our values. They are as follows:

1. Aware of the violence in the world and of the power of nonviolent resistance, I stand in the presence of ancestors, the earth, and future generations, and vow to cultivate the compassion that seeks to protect each living being.

2. Aware of the poverty and greed in the world and of the intrinsic abundance of the earth, I stand in the presence of ancestors, the earth, and future generations and vow to cultivate the simplicity, gratitude, and generosity that have no limits.

3. Aware of the abuse and lovelessness in the world and of the healing that is made possible when we open to love, I stand in the presence of the ancestors, the earth, and future generations and vow to cultivate respect for beauty and the erotic power of our bodies.

4. Aware of the falsehood and deception in the world and of the power of living and speaking the truth, I stand in the presence of the ancestors, the earth, and future generations and vow to cultivate the ability to listen, and to practice clarity and integrity in all that I communicate—by my words and my actions.

5. Aware of the contamination and desecration of the world and of my responsibility for life as it manifests through me, I stand in the presence of the ancestors, the earth, and future generations and vow to cultivate care and right action, and

to honor and respect health and well-being for my body, my mind, and the planet.

Each of us navigates our life with principles—whether consciously or unconsciously. The five precepts are keys to my map of belonging—I reflect on them personally and in community regularly. My commitments to honor life, be generous, respect erotic power, communicate honestly, and cultivate clarity are the foundation of my being. Remembering these values as I ground, know, love, and connect myself guides my belonging regardless of how tumultuous the waves and how challenging the waters.

Waves do come.

Being Includes Dying

Those of you who have lost nearests and dearests know the profundity of bereavement. My mother died in November 2016, ten days after *that* election—not a great autumn. Since then, I have had many arcs of grieving. I continue to process psychological and emotional nuances of the complex relationship I had with my mother. I am still releasing the pain and also remembering to remember the love. My ability to feel *at* all helps me feel *it* all—all the pain and all the love—accepting every aspect of being human.

Buddhism identifies three experiences of life—illness, old age, and death—that, if accepted, help us live with more freedom. Most people fear getting sick or old or dying, but when we are not in contention with these three aspects of being born, we can release our fear, leaving us free to experience joy in living. Only one of these three is inevitable for every person, because although some of us are blessed with good health for a long time and some of us will never make it to old age, every single one of us will die. Yet, our culture avoids or outright denies this reality, upholding the impossible ideal of eternal youth (and limitless success and accumulation). It's not that we need to be morbidly anti-life, retreating to await death with an insistent expectancy. Yes, we take care of ourselves (and enjoy life) while living. Self-love is all-love. Self-care is mature and wise as it benefits us and those around us. But how much can we diet, dye, CrossFit, pump, plump, inject, extract, and spurn anything that reminds us of the inevitability of dying?

Something that has helped me reconcile the inevitable changes of life (and death) is the five daily recollections. These are chanted daily in many Buddhist communities. When I was in treatment for cancer, I said them aloud to myself every morning as a reminder that what I was experiencing was neither mistake nor punishment but rather the exact measure of my humanity. They go like this:

1. I am of the nature to grow old. I have not gone beyond aging.

2. I am of the nature to be ill. I have not gone beyond illness.

3. I am of the nature to die. I have not gone beyond death.

4. All that is mine, beloved and pleasing, will change and vanish.

5. I am the owner of my actions, heir to my actions, born of my actions, related to my actions, supported by my actions. Whatever actions I do, whether wise or unwise, of that I shall be the heir.

The first three reflections on aging, illness, and death helped me deal with cancer, its uncertainty, and its aftermath. In the space of ten years I underwent three diagnoses, multiple surgeries, various treatment interventions, and permanent physical damage, all while working full-time and attending to life beyond medical trauma. The fourth reflection on what we lose did not prepare me for what came the year after my last diagnosis. Not even stage four cancer impacted me like my mother's death.

It's October 27, 2016. My birthday. Like every year on this date for the previous twenty years, I call my mother. Since she and my sister moved back to Addis Ababa in the mid-nineties, I always call right when I get up on my birthday because it's cheaper for me to call her than for her to call me. Although she's someone who is constantly misplacing the cell phone she's had for almost a decade, she inevitably has it nearby on this date, eagerly anticipating my call. And she always says the same thing after wishing me a happy birthday. "Please, Sebene, take some money from my account and go have a nice dinner somewhere." Or she tells me to buy myself a pair of shoes. She doesn't think I have nice shoes (she's right).

On this day, my cousin Ayu answers my mom's cell. Her voice is shaking, "Sebeneye, I have some bad news, my dear. *Eteye* [Aunt] Koki is in the hospital. She had a stroke this morning. You should come as soon as you can." There are only a few moments in my entire life that I remember as visceral emotional shock. Receiving my first and second and third cancer diagnoses reverberated somatically with a profound impact on my system. For me, emotional shock feels like the entire front of my body has been struck by a sonic force. The information limits my capacity for taking anything else in, for moving forward. Hearing my cousin's voice feels like that. My chest feels hit. I am immobilized for minutes. I can't think clearly. Tears begin streaming and barely stop for the next few hours.

I scramble to find a plane ticket to Ethiopia for the next day and spend a week in Addis with Ayu shuttling me between the hospital, various government agencies, and the Ethiopian Airlines office trying to obtain the paperwork to transfer my mom to a stroke center in London. She is uncommunicative and paralyzed on her right side. She's fed through a feeding tube. One week after her stroke, on November 4, we land in London. She suffers another stroke and a heart attack the day we arrive.

My mother never regained her capacity to speak or communicate. She never walked again. We were unsure what she understood. But she was not without her spirit. When Frederic arrived in London a week later, she sobbed at the sight of us together standing at the side of her bed. She went through one entire day of extreme crankiness and obstinance—states of hers not unfamiliar to me. She pulled her feeding tubes out—three times. She defiantly dropped anything I tried to place in her working hand. She batted away my caresses or attempts to do her hair or massage her neck. Speaking on the phone to her best friend, I expressed my frustration with her irritated moods. Mulalem said, "Well, you know how your mom is, that might be a good sign. Maybe she's coming back to herself." A day later, she showed a loving side also familiar to me. Looking directly in my eyes for the first time since Addis Ababa, she slowly stroked my face. A week after the elections, on November 17, 2016, exactly three weeks after my forty-sixth birthday, my mom, Koki Menkir, passed away in the ICU at Wellington Hospital in St. John's Wood, London. My sister arrived the next day expecting to see her.

Witnessing my mother's death was one of the hardest moments of my life. So was telling my sister about it.

Finot's *Maranasati*

Finot lived with our mother her entire life, never having spent more than a week apart from her. One month shy of fifty when our mother died, Finot's existence centered around Koki's for half a century. They were closer than many married couples I know. When my mom died, I became Finot's legal guardian and she lived with me and Frederic for one year until we found a living situation with which we all felt comfortable (more on that soon). Caring for her, I participated in her grieving process, and she shaped mine. Finot has the language skills and intellectual capacity of a young child. Her way of understanding our mom's death differed from mine. Her process may seem less complex (or complicated), but it contains profound lessons in belonging to life.

In the days and weeks after our mom died, Finot engaged us in a daily ritual, sometimes multiple times a day. It went something like this:

FINOT: Mommy died.

ME: Yes. Mommy died.

FINOT: Tsige [our aunt who passed away over ten years ago] died.

ME: Yes, Tsige died.

FINOT: Abate [our uncle who died over twenty years ago] too.

ME: Yes.

FINOT: Michael Jackson died.

ME: Yup, Michael Jackson died.

FINOT: Elvis died.

ME: Yes, Elvis is dead.

This process would go on to include the list of everyone who Finot could remember had died. Luckily, it's not an outrageously long list, but it still could go on for quite a while. It included random seventies TV personalities (using the character names, not the actors') as well as old family friends I'd completely forgotten. Sometimes one of us would correct her: *No, Finot, Stevie Wonder is not dead.* We did this multiple times a day. Every day. For weeks. But, wait—there's more.

After we completed the list of everyone who already died, we would start the process of naming everyone we know would die. Which. Is. Every. Damn. One.

FINOT: Stevie Wonder, he's going to die.

ME: Yes, unfortunately, Stevie Wonder will die.

FINOT: Asgede's going to die.

ME: Yes. Asgede will die.

FINOT: Suki [our dog] too.

ME: Yes, Suki too.

FINOT: Freddy is going to die.

ME: Yup, even Freddy.

FINOT: Obama's gonna die.

ME: Yes . . .

This process is longer. And quite sobering. I was describing all of this to my friend Erin who stated, "That's *maraṇasati*." Yes, indeed it is.

As we've explored, in the Satipatthana Sutta, the first foundation of mindfulness is of the body. Included in contemplation of the body are mindfulness of breathing, the body in its various activities, and the four elements of air, water, earth, and fire. Mindfulness of the body also includes the body's anatomical parts. The final contemplation in mindfulness of the body is *maraṇasati*, or death awareness. The formal practice includes a contemplation of the deceased, decaying body (classically, practitioners are instructed to visit charnel grounds). The ultimate insight of this practice is truly understanding the inevitability of death. Finot helped us practice that every day, over and over.

Our delusional attempts to avoid the inevitable truth of impermanence will not save us—accumulating more stuff that won't last is not the answer, neither is hating our aging bodies. An intentional and regular contemplation of death is a radical meditation in a culture that teaches us to abhor death, glorify youth, and to (unsuccessfully) defy aging. Finot's meditation is right. None of us are getting out of this alive. Not even Obama. Yet many of our anxieties and fears are founded on denial of this simple truth. *We be. Then, we die.*

Finot's death meditations became lighter as the months passed, even playful. Our *maraṇasati* became mostly about gratitude.

FINOT: Mommy died.

ME: Yes. Mommy died.

FINOT: She's gone.

ME: Yup.

FINOT: She's dead. Kaput. Finito. No more. So long. Bye. [waves to the sky]

ME: [giggle]

FINOT: I miss my mother so much. Mommy is the nicest person in the whole world.

Oh Despair:
Some Sun Has Got to Rise

Falling might very well be flying—without the tyranny of coordinates.
—BAYO AKOMOLAFE

It's true that dominant culture encourages us to live in denial of death so we can consume all things young (also: the youths have more buying days ahead—so they matter more to capitalism). Nonetheless, as planetary crises consume our consciousness, many of us grapple with the prospect of collective death on a daily basis. We anxiously witness wildfires, floods, extreme temperature changes, species extinction, global pandemics, and general ecological disaster. We feel powerless against the structural violence perpetrated through war, extraordinary inequality, as well as institutionalized racism, misogyny, ableism, xenophobia, homophobia, and transphobia and the many resulting interpersonal acts of harm these and other systems beget. Whether or not we believe that humanity is on the brink of extinction (I'm not so sure), it's clear that life on this planet is shifting unalterably and many beings (human and non) will perish along the way. Meditation only helps right now.

Edward Conze, a noted historian of Buddhism, explains that according to ancient commentary *"two only* among the forty meditational practices are always and under all circumstances beneficial—*the development of friendliness, and the recollection of death"* [emphasis mine]. The Buddha offered forty practices but only two (5 percent!) are applicable all the time. If we are paying attention, we're already contemplating the demise of many things (if we're not, time to wake up!). That means our primary challenge is to balance thinking about death with developing friendliness toward life. In the midst of these crises, we must *be ourselves* without succumbing to despair.

As you've come to expect, I am speaking to myself. Since the 2016 election and gearing up to 2020's inevitable political shit show, each catastrophic new event and news cycle (hello, un-expected global pandemic!) can stir within me feelings of despair, even a loss of faith in the future. The strange truth is that many things are better today than let's say five, ten, or even a hundred years ago—for Black people, the LGBTQI community, women, Africa, the concept of democracy (going too far back, let's say to 1492, negates this theory). Although modernity and colonialism devastated cultures, there have been correctives to those forces. In many places, there is actually less violence, crime, war, and exploitation. Some even say we may be living in the most peaceful period in the history of our species. This is not to say things are okay. There are avowed white supremacists planning and perpetrating harm. Young women are still sold into sexual slavery. The Earth herself is not okay. There is a lot of not-okayness in the world! But today we are both privileged and saddled with the perpetual awareness of what is happening on the other side of the planet (and the appropriate longing to stop injustices often done in our names).

Seeing certain things clearly doesn't mean we are seeing everything clearly. I imagine if you're reading this book, you are not irretrievably lost in the rabbit hole of consumerism that encourages ignorance of injustice. However, we can often be trapped in another hole—that of the endless scroll of outraged social media posts, nonstop news coverage, expert analysis, inexpert opinions, uncivil disagreements, and inflammatory comment threads. All of this overamplifies our awareness of the negative. Many of us experienced this with the coronavirus pandemic and recent uprisings in defense of Black lives. I certainly had to will myself to stop reading the news incessantly and give myself space to contemplate things beyond crisis or consciously take in the numerous positive actions that were arising in response.

Despair can be an appropriate response to horror. It is understandable that we flirt with hopelessness when confronted with unbridled greed, hatred, and ignorance. And our meditation practice teaches us the difference between an appropriate response and a habitual reaction. Other stuff is happening. Good stuff. Powerful stuff. We can seek it out by unsubscribing and disconnecting from bad news and identifying good information (I suggest David Byrne's *Reasons to Be Cheerful*). We can also go outside, be with friends, get intimate with life itself. When I connect to the natural world, I am reminded that the sun keeps rising and billions of animals keep engaging in natural cycles. When I have friends over for dinner (even by Zoom), we can linger and laugh and lament in a way that's not possible in a crowded restaurant. If I stay mired in despair, I'm not responding to life any longer: I'm wallowing. And I'm wallowing in the culture's thoughts. My attention has been hijacked. My being is held hostage.

The Buddha said whatever we frequently think and ponder upon will become the inclination of our minds. When I pay attention, I notice that the inclination of my mind affects my feelings, emotions, moods, conversations, decisions, actions . . . my life. The news (and my social media feed) can incline my mind to only think about disaster, pandemics, violence, fear, celebrity absurdity, and election nonsense. But life changes with each moment. Images of murder and devastation are followed by feeling a gentle breeze from the window pass over the tops of my legs. Worries about a loved one are accompanied by the sound of a buzzing bee caught between the screen and window. I can choose the inclination of my mind. The Yeah Yeah Yeahs put it like this:

> *Oh despair, you've always been there...*
> *If it's all in my head there's nothing to fear*
> *Nothing to fear inside*
> *Through the darkness and the light*
> *Some sun has got to rise*

Some sun has got to rise. Remember, "creative" and "reactive" are the same letters and curiosity is the key. A true response is momentary. Reactivity is perpetuated by a thinking mind that is locked into concepts or perceptions, closed off to the changing moments of lived experience, no longer curious. I don't need to push despair away, but I do need to take responsibility not to get stuck in its loop (which probably entails taking many, many breaks from the news, email, and social media). In any moment, I can choose to be in a different response, a creative response. Breath by breath.

Intimacy and Imagination: A Conspiracy of Consciousness

We die. That may be the meaning of life. But we do language. That may be the measure of our lives.
—TONI MORRISON

Never underestimate the power of a deep inhale and a deep exhale. Breath is at the center of so many sacred practices. We can live more than fifty days without food and around seven days without water, but without oxygen we cannot survive more than about five minutes. The breath is one of the most unique processes in the body: it is internal and external, it is both voluntary and involuntary, it balances the sympathetic nervous system and parasympathetic nervous system, and it fosters empathetic attunement—we tend to breathe in harmony with those to whom we feel connected. Whether we want to or not, we share our breath with every breathing being around us. Molecules within me have been within you. Whether it's other mammals breathing oxygen or trees breathing in our carbon dioxide, breath connects.

Researcher Ralph Keeling has recently shown that only about half of our oxygen comes from terrestrial plants. The rest is made by algae and bacteria in lakes and oceans, with a small additional measure produced by the sun and distant stars (we are breathing galactic oxygen!). He deduced that the oxygen we breathe mixes throughout each respective hemisphere within two months and spreads worldwide in a little more than a year. We are literally breathing the breath of all the beings on the planet every year. We inhale and exhale all that also breathes. But not just living now. As abundant as atoms are on this planet, their numbers are finite. In fact, we are breathing with the breath of all that has ever lived.

The list is endless of those with whom we have breathed—all the characters of history (heroes and villains alike), all the beings known and unknown, remembered and forgotten. We are *breathing with* each other. We are not and never have been separate. We are breathing with the dinosaurs, with every ocean wave and gentle breeze, with all of our ancestors, with Nefertiti and St. Theresa, with Patrice Lumumba and the Buddha, with all the atoms and all the dimensions, with the sunrises of millions of years, with the mystery and the spirit. You can feel it for yourself right now— breathe with, con-spire.

The word "conspiracy" caught my attention many years ago when I went to see *Lumumba* with my friend Noel. The film follows the true story of the rise and death of the Congolese leader. Standing in line for tickets, Noel and I lamented a mainstream reviewer describing Lumumba's assassination as a "conspiracy theory." "*Theory?*" Noel and I asked ourselves in vain. The CIA conspired to kill Lumumba. That's not a "theory," it's well-documented fact (only officially uncovered many years after his death). I was newly enamored with etymology and ignorant (still am) of Latin, so, later that night I was delighted to discover that "conspiracy" translates to "breathe with." *Con* means "with" and *spire* is related to "breath," also to "spirit." To conspire is to be with each other's breath or essence. Or, when desecrated, to take life. Lumumba's assassins (and the ones who plotted his death— Eisenhower and the British and Belgian governments) certainly breathed with each other in person or over scratchy midcentury telephone lines while plotting to murder the first democratically elected leader of the Congo. There have been countless conspiracies, smaller and larger, against life, before and since (BTW, mainstream news and *New York Times* movie reviews will *not* tell you about most of them). There are conspiracies being enacted right now to harm some of the most vulnerable people in our society. There are conspiracies—this is *not* theory. Those conspiracies can make us feel powerless. But we *do* have power. As Santee Dakota activist John Trudell said,

> We have power. . . . Our power isn't in a political system, or a religious system, or in an economic system, or in a military system; these are authoritarian systems . . . they have power . . . but it's not reality. The power of our intelligence, individually or collectively *is* the power; this is the power that any industrial ruling class truly fears: clear coherent human beings.

Why was Lumumba killed? Because he was organizing and ener-gizing the people and threatening the control of resources. The same reason Martin Luther King Jr., Fred Hampton, and others were killed—because *they* were breathing together in the margins—cultivating people's spirit, their inherent power of interconnection, and the right to not be exploited. They aspired ("aspire" also origi-nates from *spire*) to teach us all that we belong.

Can we aspire together? Can we conspire together? Actually, we must. We need to breathe together in a conspiracy of consciousness.

We *do* have power. We each have the power of being and belong-ing. That power needs to be nurtured and cultivated, individually and collectively. Every day. We are not the same; we can begin to understand our personal and collective conditioning and, in spite of this, reclaim our belonging to each other, to everything. We are not separate; we can cultivate collective conscious values, con-scious commitments, and conscious aspirations.

But how? How do we breathe together in a way that honors our conscious aspirations for equality and freedom, for kindness and care? How do we breathe together to resist the agendas of very real and harmful conspiracies? How do we breathe together in the consciousness that is absolutely fundamental, that is sacred and universal?

We *do* it through intimacy and imagination, through *being*.

A friend was lamenting to me recently that they did not get enough work done over a holiday week. This person did not have deadlines they would miss or anyone to disappoint by taking a weekend (or week or even two) off. It was simply an inner critic relentlessly cri-tiquing their inadequate output. How many of us feel like that about our vacations, weekends, evenings, daily commute, the last ten minutes? We feel compelled to constantly be doing.

Being is lost in the pressure of activity (and accumulation). For many of us, our work, livelihood, and self-worth are wrapped up not only in doing but also constantly communicating *about* all our doing—we feel compelled to post about what we just did. The pathology of productivity is entwined with a pathology of performativity. The need to always do (and share) keeps us from grounding, knowing, loving, connecting, and ultimately from being. The internet is not the enemy, but our attention and energy have been hijacked to the point where we can't exist without constant activity. Productivity and performativity deprive us of intimacy and imagination.

Intimacy involves an embodied awareness of what's happening within us and in relationship to the world. We cannot be intimate if we are continually in motion (physically or mentally), if we cannot take the time to simply feel. We become intimate with ourselves and others through being. Imagination invites the opportunity to respond clearly and creatively to each moment. Imagination allows for the possibility of new ways. We cannot create what we cannot imagine. Lumumba imagined a different way. Someone else imagined Lumumba's death.

If we want a different world, we must imagine it. To imagine it, we must become intimate with our deepest wishes. We cannot imagine without a desire for creation, without longing for something different. We cannot connect to our deepest desire without simply being. We cannot long if we can't feel what it is we long for. Try it right now:

Close your eyes, become intimate with your breath, and let yourself be. Take a few deep inhales and exhales.

Now consider this: *What do you most long for? Can you imagine it?*

We *be* so we can *long*. In the process we can become our longing. Being invites the intimacy and imagination that lead to belonging.

I Am, Therefore I Be: Belonging Is the Answer

*[Be . . .] The entire essence of language is
concentrated in that singular word.*

—MICHEL FOUCAULT

Camphill Village is a community one hundred miles north of New York City in Copake, New York, where adults with developmental and intellectual disabilities and a diverse group of volunteers live and work together as equals in extended family homes. The Camphill movement was started by Dr. Karl König, an Austrian pediatrician who fled Nazi occupation of his country and along with others started the first Camphill community for children in Aberdeen, Scotland, in 1939. Together they integrated the teachings of Rudolf Steiner to develop the philosophy that underlies Camphill communities around the world (over one hundred in more than twenty countries): that if each member of a community can contribute their gifts and talents, the needs of all can be met in cooperation.

Finot had been living with us for over six months when I first told her about the Camphill in Copake. Months earlier, Frederic and I had left Finot with a friend and visited there. Sitting with her now, I asked if I could show her the video on their website, explaining to her that Frederic and I had seen and really liked it. If she agreed, we would take her there for a tour. She tensed up immediately. I expected that. I knew she might feel hurt or afraid by the idea of leaving us. We hadn't talked about the future, but she may have assumed she would live with me and Frederic "forever." We ourselves had considered that possibility until my friend Tod mentioned a community he volunteered for one town over from his in the Hudson Valley. On our first visit, we were shown around by a staff member and a "villager" (a special needs resident). I don't have the words to describe how impressed we were. In all the decades I had pondered Finot's fate, the years I implored my mom to consider or plan for Finot's care after her death, I had never once imagined a place like Camphill. But someone had imagined it.

Camphill Village is an integrated community, meaning people with disabilities live and work together cooperatively with short- and long-term volunteers. The village population includes about one hundred villagers, an equal number of volunteers (called co-workers), and dozens of children (of long-term co-workers). Many of the current villagers and co-workers have lived there for decades, and some are retired residents. There are a small number of staff members who work in the offices who do not live at Camphill, but otherwise villagers and co-workers exist in a symbiotic daily and seasonal flow. There is an organic, biodynamic farm that grows vegetables and raises animals for dairy, eggs, and meat; a bakery that bakes all the bread for the village; and a healing plant garden that cultivates herbs and plants for teas, tinctures, and salves. In addition, products are created for use in the village and for sale in the gift shop through a number of workshops including: a weavery, a candle shop, a woodshop, a seedery, a bookbindery, and a stained-glass shop. Maple trees on the six-hundred-plus acres are tapped for syrup and processed in a sugar house, and the land and buildings are maintained by an estate crew. Residents maintain these activities as well as administrative roles. Everyone has morning and afternoon duties, with homes being another location where someone can work. There are twenty-one simple but beautiful houses, each accommodating between eight and twelve people, and villagers and co-workers cook and clean together to feed and accommodate the meals and needs of everyone. Houses are spread out across the property and clustered into "neighborhoods" of three homes with gardens, farmland, workshops, a co-op (general) store, a café, a gift shop, a meeting hall, and other buildings distributed throughout.

Telling Finot about all of this in our apartment office (which had become her bedroom), I said what I had rehearsed on a call with my teacher Kittisaro: "Finot, you know I love you and I only want the very best for you, right? I just want you to consider Camphill. If you don't like it or you don't want to go, that's fine. I just want you to think about it. Can you trust me?" We watched the video and Finot tearily agreed to a visit.

On the day of Finot's "interview," she was quiet on the car ride up the Taconic Parkway. Finot is extremely outgoing, the extrovert in the family. She is also very brave, always willing to try every roller coaster and ride at an amusement park. She was happy to meet people in the conference room for the admissions meeting. But she was surprised when after fifteen minutes, a volunteer arrived to take her on a tour while Frederic and I stayed behind to be interviewed. Still, she was amiable as she went off to see the village and tour the workshops and activities. When she came back forty minutes later, she was beaming. "Sebene, it's niiiice here. They got cows and chickens and, and . . . everything."

After we went home and the three of us discussed it as a family, Finot agreed to the monthlong trial visit required for admission. It must be a mutual decision between an applicant and the community that moving to Camphill Village is a good idea. Finot would spend a month trying different workshop assignments and understanding the routines and rhythms of life there. For the month of October, almost a year after our mother's death, Finot stayed in Hickory House with two longtime co-workers and their children (a married straight Israeli couple with three teenage sons), two younger short-term co-workers (one from Germany and one from China), and five intellectually disabled adults (one who had lived in the village almost fifty years—practically since its founding in 1961).

As we drove up to the driveway on Finot's move-in day, one of Finot's villager-housemates was walking home from work up to the house with a bouquet of wildflowers (probably from the healing plant garden) to give her as a welcome gift. The hospitality extended inside where the door to Finot's bedroom for the month was decorated with a colorful welcome sign. She can only recognize a few written words, her first name being the primary one. She was so happy to see that on entering her small but tidy and sun-filled room.

She teared up a bit when we left that Monday, but by our weekend check-in call she was jubilant. Finot's trial month was a huge success. She loved the Camphill community, the various workshops she tried, and the many friends she made in those four weeks. She experienced a level of independence she had never had in her life. Life in the village is very structured, with mealtimes and work hours set collectively, but free time throughout each day and on the weekends allowed her to go to the café, take walks, attend activities, and visit with people as she pleased. When I reflected on this first taste of autonomy for her, it reminded me of when I was getting ready to go away to college at the age of seventeen. Finot was twenty-one and aging out of her special needs public school in DC and seemed anxious about me leaving home. When she would get sad about my impending departure, my mother would tell her, "Finot, it's okay, maybe you can go to college one day, too." This would somehow ease Finot's worries, which always struck me as odd. In my estimation of her abilities, I assumed she wanted me to stay, not that she longed to leave. Now I recognize that, even all those years ago, she may have longed for independence, too.

Finot decided she definitely wanted to move to Camphill. We waited for a spot to open and in January, she moved into Argo House, a home with four co-workers and four other villagers. Every weekday morning, after breakfast and cleanup, she walks to another home where she helps prep food and cook for their meals. After, she returns home for lunch or goes to lunch at another house if she's invited out. Before she goes to her afternoon shift in the seed shop, she has free time, which she often uses to listen to CDs or to draw. Turtle Tree Seed is a workshop and successful business that offers over 385 varieties of open-pollinated, Demeter-certified Biodynamic® vegetable, flower, and herb seeds. Finot helps to grow, select, and clean the seeds. This is what her bio says about her on their website:

Finot started at Turtle Tree in 2018 when she moved to Camphill Village. She always comes to work with a cheerful spirit and keeps the whole crew on track with her strong work ethic and enthusiasm. Finot works both in the gardens and helping to clean seed.

The intimacy and imagination of Camphill provide Finot the space to be exactly as she is and contribute in ways she never experienced before. She engages in meaningful work, creative activities (on Thursday evenings, she goes to her drum group), a rich spiritual life, and a variety of relationships. She embodies the power of *being* as belonging. Last summer, Finot went on her first trip without family: a two-week tour of Iceland. The group of co-workers and villagers went whale watching, visited hot springs, went hiking, and stayed at Sólheimar, a lifesharing community similar to Camphill. When I went to Camphill to see her after she got back, she excitedly handed me a wrapped box. After years of people bringing her souvenirs from their trips, she had proudly picked out a beautiful black lava stone necklace that I wear now almost every day.

Camphill Village is one of thousands of intentional communities around the world. Each one has been imagined by people who dared to explore their power to create new ways of being on this Earth. Our current planetary crisis is the result of innumerable moments of individual and collective experience. Most of us will not live in a community like Camphill, but each of us can cultivate our capacity to live in ways that honor our inherent interconnection. Through intimacy and imagination we can consciously create the world we live in together. Through belonging, we connect to ourselves, each other, and everything and, ultimately, remember what we are. We are freedom. We are joy. We are love. We belong.

Ten Tips for Meditating at Home

Create Space

Eventually, you can have many spaces or no particular spot, but, in the beginning, designate one place in your home for meditation. You don't need to invest in special cushions or clear an entire room or even a corner. You can meditate on your bed, on a chair, lying down, sitting up, cross-legged or not. But do choose that one seat, posture, cushion, scarf, or object to signify your meditation practice. Making it pretty and peaceful helps signal to the mind and body that this is good for you.

Schedule a Regular Time

Try to meditate at roughly the same time at least four to five times a week. Choose a time that works with your daily routine. For many people, first thing in the morning is best, before you've been sucked into any responsibilities (emailing, getting kids up, making breakfast). But any time that works for you is perfect. Put it in your calendar and let your roommates, partner, workmates, or kids know that you are unplugged for that period (and that they will also benefit from you being calmer and kinder).

Start Small

Don't set yourself up for failure with unrealistic expectations like meditating one full hour every day. It's much more powerful to meditate for ten minutes five days a week than for one hour twice a month. Think of meditation like strength training (for your brain). A few push-ups every day will yield more results than lifting a really heavy dumbbell a single time—in the beginning five or ten "push-ups" will be your max.

Airplane Mode Is Your Ally

Yes, most of us will use our smartphone to time our meditation period. *Do not* let notification settings ruin this; it's already hard enough to build a meditation practice. Use an offline timer if you can or at least put your gadget in airplane mode. Give yourself this break from connectivity and know that meditation is shown to off-set all that (over)stimulation.

Settle into Your Body

Get comfortable. Meditation is a balance between being alert (paying attention to your experience) and being relaxed (gently releasing any tension and letting go of stories). If you are sitting, make sure your back is straight (but not rigid) and your chest is open. Relax your arms and hands in your lap or on your knees. You want to be able to maintain a reasonable amount of stillness for the entire period, so make sure nothing feels strained or pinched. Better yet, lie down!

Find an Anchor

The breath is a common focus or anchor in mindfulness meditation. It makes a great object for attention because it's always there. Find somewhere in the body to follow the breath; the belly/diaphragm or the nostrils/nose are common places. Experiment with what's easiest and most relaxed, but stick with one place to follow the breath for each meditation period. This is your anchor when thoughts distract you, but . . .

Thoughts Are Not the Enemy

Many people think meditation is about stopping thoughts—well, good luck with that. The mind thinks: that's its job. Mindfulness meditation is helping us unhook from our tendency to get caught up in thoughts without any conscious awareness. The first time you meditate, you might notice the instructions are simple (be with the breath in the present moment) but the practice is difficult (you keep getting lost in thinking about the past or future). The key is to remember that getting caught up in thoughts is normal. Just make note of thinking and return to the breath (over and over again). In the beginning, you might only be able to follow one breath; you are training, just like with those push-ups.

Working with Noise Sounds and Pain Sensations

You might have a picture of the ideal meditation situation: practicing meditation in a silent, serene meditation room with no noise and the perfect ergonomic meditation seat. But mindfulness meditation is helping you be less reactive to your life, and life includes unwelcome sounds and unpleasant sensations; try not to think of these as noise or pain. If the situation is intolerable, change positions or close the window. Otherwise, make note of sound or sensation and return to the breath.

Mindfulness Is About Remembering (and Kindness)

You will get caught up in thoughts. Even experienced meditators do. The challenge is remembering to practice and remembering to return to the breath . . . and not beating yourself up when you forget about either (which you will, about both, again and again). Pay particular attention to the moment you notice you were "lost"

—this itself is a moment of mindfulness. Often we judge ourselves for being lost, but this is actually a moment to bring some ease and even a little celebration: *I woke up! Hurrah!* Pay attention to how it feels. Ease and happiness grow with our ability to meet experience with some sense of kindness and clarity. You're learning something new, give yourself a break: celebrate the awakenings (and give it some time).

Use Resources

Guided meditations and community can be helpful, especially for new meditators. Here are a few apps to get you started (note, I teach on the first two):

Ten Percent Happier has diverse teachers, meditations, and courses for the basics and beyond—and you can do a seven-day intro course for free.

Liberate is an app by and for the Black and African Diaspora that features a number of POC teachers.

Insight Timer is rated as the top free meditation app on the Android and iOS stores. You can also connect to people around the world in groups that meditate together virtually.

Journal Prompts & Meditations and Practice

The Delusion of Separation: We Were Never Separate

JOURNAL PROMPTS

What does belonging mean to me? To whom or what have I felt I belonged or not belonged in my life?

What is evoked for me by the idea that we are not separate? What about the idea that we are not the same?

What margins or centers do I occupy? When and how did I understand these social locations?

MEDITATION AND PRACTICE

If you have a meditation practice, please continue. If you are new to meditation, at least four times this week, take ten minutes to sit in a comfortable posture and simply be with your experience in stillness and silence. Set a timer. Feel free to use an app or a guided meditation. Notice how this is for you.

Domination: Fueling the Fire of Not Belonging

JOURNAL PROMPTS

List memories of comparison or competition in your life (gold stars, contests, trophies, weighing yourself, grade point averages, test scores, sales rankings, performance evaluations, etc.). How have these impacted you?

MEDITATION AND PRACTICE

Continue cultivating a daily meditation practice.

When you are in a public place where you can watch people (e.g., café, park, or subway) notice how you categorize, compare, and/or compete with others. What evaluations are you making: greater than, less than, equal to? Remember, *mana* is with us until the end. We are simply loosening its most tenacious and egregious forms. See if you can let go of any shame or blame for the thoughts that mirror the hierarchy and domination of our society.

Ground Yourself

JOURNAL PROMPTS

Stop three times each day (e.g., at noon, end of workday, and just before bed) and ask yourself the following questions (take brief notes to notice patterns):

How connected am I to my body in this moment?

How can I tell?

Any other observations about this?

MEDITATION AND PRACTICE

In your meditation practice, notice: What sensations are pleasant? Unpleasant? Neutral? Explore staying with these experiences without a need to grasp or reject anything. What do you notice? For five minutes, pay attention only to what is easeful or pleasant in your body. Bring your full awareness to this ease. Allow yourself to savor this pleasure.

Explore what brings you pleasure throughout the day. Allow yourself to savor sensations and experiences that bring you pleasure.

DANCE! Put on a favorite song, go to a dance class, or go dancing with friends. How long, where, or when does not matter. Just dance.

Know Yourself

JOURNAL PROMPTS

Where are your people from? What do you know about your ancestors? If there are gaps in your knowledge, is there anyone you can ask? If not, can you do a little research about the general information you have (e.g., if you are adopted, research your country or culture of origin and learn about the beliefs and practices of the place)?

How would you describe yourself to a new friend? To a new colleague? To a stranger?

What parts of yourself do you see? What parts of yourself do you not want to see?

MEDITATION AND PRACTICE

In your daily meditation practice, pay attention to your particular patterns. Where does your awareness tend to go: to the future or past, to worry or obsession, to planning or control, to fantasy or dreaminess? No need to change anything, just notice the patterns.

Love Yourself

JOURNAL PROMPTS

What messages did you receive about what is good or allowable about you? What was considered bad or not allowable? How were you encouraged to be? What was rewarded? What was discouraged? Did you accept these messages? Did you internalize them? Did you rebel against any of them?

Notice your inner committee today. Who is sitting on it? What do they have to say? Do you believe them?

MEDITATION AND PRACTICE

Start a gratitude practice. Every day write down three things for which you are grateful—try to include things about yourself from time to time. Use a journal or start a message chain with one or more friends.

Connect Yourself

JOURNAL PROMPTS

What can you disconnect from? What is absolutely necessary? What do you hold on to out of a sense of obligation/guilt/decorum/fear? What are you willing to drop? And what happens when you do? To whom and to what do you connect when you make space?

MEDITATION AND PRACTICE

Take a break from all technology! Here are some suggestions:

> Don't bring any tech into your bedroom at night (get a "real" alarm clock) and don't go online until after you meditate in the morning. (This is a personal favorite!)

> Designate certain times of the day when you and/or your family are off all tech: mealtimes, family outings, walks in nature. (You can get selfies at other times.)

> Create a weekly Tech Sabbath—an entire day where you do not go online.

> Put your Wi-Fi on a timer (like those used for lamps when you go on vacation) and have it go off one hour before your bedtime and on one hour after you wake (another personal favorite).

A stand of aspen trees is actually one large organism where the roots are a single life force. From a standing position, imagine all the people and beings currently in your life as a field of aspen trees. Locating yourself among this field, sense your feet rooted into the ground and connecting with a root system that connects you to all of the other trees. Now imagine that this root system is connected not only to those you know and love but to every single being and entity known and unknown. Stand tall. There is air and space around you but everything is connected underneath, within. Can you feel space and contact? Can you feel independent and connected?

Be Yourself

JOURNAL PROMPTS

Can you allow yourself to open to the mystery of you? Your everyday life? What stops you? Are you too rushed? Are you too busy to appreciate with wonder and awe those flowers by the window?

What inspires awe in you? Can you allow yourself more opportunities to witness a sunset from start to finish (and when does it start and when does it finish?)?

MEDITATION AND PRACTICE

Do less. I dare you. Saying no, letting go of obligations, cancelling appointments, staying off social media—these can feel like revolutionary acts. They often are. Try it.

Appreciate the miracle of this moment. That you are sitting/standing/lying here right now, breathing, pulsing, reading, understanding. And that millions of years of evolution led to right now. What does that feel like? What do you notice?

ACKNOWLEDGMENTS

Thank you to the Earth and all her beings, both seen and unseen, and to the elements and forces to which I have always belonged. Thank you to my ancestors for thriving and adapting so I can belong today. To my mother Koki Menkir and father Bereket Habte Selassie, I owe the gift of life. To the Buddhadharma, I owe waking up to this life.

So many people have impacted me along my journey to writing this book. I cannot include them all here. Please know that I appreciate everyone who I have met along my many paths of belonging. To those who showed up when I was frighteningly sick—Ahmad Azadi, Amanda Tobier, Betsy Guttmacher, Katherine Dore, Siobhan Roth—I can never thank you enough. To the over 450 people who donated money to help me in a time of great need, I am forever grateful.

Thank you to my agent, Anna Geller, for first reaching out and graciously accompanying me every step of the way. Your wise and warm counsel steadies me. To my editor, Sydney Rogers, your enthusiasm has been a beacon of bright light—thank you for championing this book from its infancy. For guidance on the proposal, I have immense gratitude for Joelle Hahn and Pam Weiss. *You Belong* could never have happened without your wise and talented input as writers. Deep bows.

Thank you to Joseph Goldstein and Sharon Salzberg for early support and inspiration. Deep gratitude to Mark Epstein for helping me believe I could write a book. Dan Harris, our conversations and your curiosity always inspire me—I deeply appreciate your ongoing support and friendship. Thank you Tara Brach for your guidance and love over many years—I've learned so much from you. Thank you to Jocelyn K. Glei for *Reset* and for helping me tune my antennae. Deep thanks to Ruth King for precious sisterhood and wise advice. To Ilan and Louisa Bohm, Kassia Frihet, and Tatiana Martushev, I am grateful for your generous and compassionate love and care. Thank you to Mike Albo for years of patient writerly advice (I took notes all along the way).

To my many cohort members, you have given me so many places and ways to belong. Thank you to my friends in CDL4, IFOT, Dharmapala, and the Feminine Dharma Conspiracy. I have immense gratitude to Shirley Turcotte for birthing Indigenous Focusing Oriented Therapy and for tirelessly manifesting this medicine across Turtle Island.

I am blessed with dharma peers who love, challenge, and inspire me. Deep appreciation to Brian Lesage, Dalila Bothwell, Erin Treat, JoAnna Hardy, and La Sarmiento. You make me a better student and teacher. Thank you to Lynn Whitmore for daily gratitude. DaRa Williams, your friendship and love has helped guide my journey; thank you sis. Allyson Pimentel, I am incredibly fortunate to have crossed paths with you in this life. Thank you for being there with divine clarity and kindness at key moments—this book could never have happened without you.

I have been blessed with many teachers over the years; I can't name them all. For your love and generosity thank you to Gloria

Taraniya Ambrosia, Eugene Cash, and Larry Yang. Thank you to Gina Sharpe for believing in me before I could believe in myself. To Thanissara and Kittisaro, my deepest gratitude for your love and guidance all these years and for the Kuan Yin Dharmas.

To my brilliant, generous, and kindhearted readers—Aaron Schultz, Rollo Romig, Shahnaz Habib, and Susa Talan—I cannot thank you enough for your energy and insights.

Thank you to Camphill Village for creating a community where everyone belongs. And to Nadege Ott and Samuel Mirkin for making Argo House a home where anyone who enters feels belonging.

To Aaron Plant and Art Faramarzi, you opened your home and hearts at a difficult moment for me personally. Your loving gen-erosity allowed this book to take shape. Thank you especially to Aaron for being the best Kitten a Kitten could ask for. To my cousin Ayehu Berhan Lemma, your unbounded love and unwavering sup-port helped me survive the most difficult moment of my life. I can never thank you enough. To Jacky Davis, Naomi Urabe, and Nicola Usborne, thank you for all the giggles and girls' trips and for always, always being there. To Peter Bird, our decades of conversations have made me a better thinker and person. Your wit and wisdom have deeply impacted these pages—thank you.

To Suki, the best dog until the very end, thank you for teaching me about unconditional belonging. I love you forever. Thank you to my brother, Asgede, for first introducing me to the dharma thirty-five years ago—it has saved my life. To my sister Finot, I love you to the moon and back. Thank you for being the best sister I could ever imagine.

To my love, Frederic, your devotion and unwavering belief in me, your insights and suggestions, and you yourself made this pos-sible. This book is ours.